52 LITTLE LESSONS FROM
A CHRISTMAS CAROL

OTHER BOOKS BY BOB WELCH

52

LITTLE LESSONS

from

A Christmas Carol

BOB WELCH

NELSON
BOOKS

An Imprint of Thomas Nelson

52 Little Lessons from A Christmas Carol

© 2021 by Bob Welch

All rights reserved. No portion of this book may be reproduced, stored in a retrieval system, or transmitted in any form or by any means—electronic, mechanical, photocopy, recording, scanning, or other—except for brief quotations in critical reviews or articles, without the prior written permission of the publisher.

Published in Nashville, Tennessee, by Thomas Nelson. Thomas Nelson is a registered trademark of HarperCollins Christian Publishing, Inc.

Thomas Nelson titles may be purchased in bulk for educational, business, fund-raising, or sales promotional use. For information, please email SpecialMarkets@ThomasNelson.com.

Unless otherwise noted, Scripture quotations are taken from the Holy Bible, New International Version®, NIV®. Copyright © 1973, 1978, 1984, 2011 by Biblica, Inc.® Used by permission of Zondervan. All rights reserved worldwide. www.zondervan.com. The "NIV" and "New International Version" are trademarks registered in the United States Patent and Trademark Office by Biblica, Inc.®

Scripture quotations marked KJV are taken from the King James Version. Public domain.

Scripture quotations marked NKJV are taken from the New King James Version®. Copyright © 1982 by Thomas Nelson. Used by permission. All rights reserved.

Any internet addresses, phone numbers, or company or product information printed in this book are offered as a resource and are not intended in any way to be or to imply an endorsement by Thomas Nelson, nor does Thomas Nelson vouch for the existence, content, or services of these sites, phone numbers, companies, or products beyond the life of this book.

ISBN 978-0-7852-6591-7 (HC)
ISBN 978-1-4002-0675-9 (eBook)
ISBN 978-0-7852-6632-7 (Audiobook)

Library of Congress Control Number: 2015936308

Printed in the United States of America

21 22 23 24 25 LSC 6 5 4 3 2 1

To those who, like Scrooge, dare to start anew

Contents

Contents

Contents

List of Characters

Ebenezer Scrooge—greedy, grumpy owner of a nineteenth-century London accounting office who is visited by three spirits bent on thawing his stone-cold heart.

Bob Cratchit—Scrooge's clerk, a lowly bean counter with a small income and a big heart. Despite Scrooge's relentless grouchiness, Cratchit remains humbly dedicated to the man and happily devoted to his family.

Fred—Scrooge's nephew, a man who gushes with Christmas spirit and steadfastly encourages his uncle to lose his bitterness, and, in essence, to join the party.

Jacob Marley—Ebenezer Scrooge's dead partner whose ghost returns seven years after Marley dies to warn the old buzzard that death is a chain-dragging hell and yet there's still time for him to change his ways.

Tiny Tim—Cratchit's small son, who's been crippled since birth.

The Ghost of Christmas Past—the first spirit to visit Scrooge, a childlike character whose head glows. It shows Scrooge the Christmases of his past.

The Ghost of Christmas Present—the second spirit to visit Scrooge, an oversized being in a green robe. It shows Scrooge the holiday celebrations of the old geezer's contemporaries.

The Ghost of Christmas Yet to Come—the third and final spirit to visit Scrooge, a silent phantom in a hooded robe. It shows Scrooge an ominous look at Ebenezer's lonely death—and, of course, the Cratchit home minus Tiny Tim.

Fezziwig—Scrooge's former boss, a lighthearted merchant who treats his employees to festive Christmas parties.

Belle—Scrooge's former love, a beautiful woman who breaks off their engagement rather than compete with Ebenezer's newfound obsession with wealth.

Fan—Scrooge's sister who dies after giving birth to Fred. Ebenezer loved her deeply.

The Portly Gentlemen—two men who seek charitable contributions from Scrooge at the story's start—and are promptly thrown out of his office.

Peter Cratchit—Bob's oldest son, who will soon make his way in the world.

Martha Cratchit—Bob's oldest daughter, who works in a hat shop.

Mrs. Cratchit—Bob's kind and loving wife.

Author's Note

How do we learn life lessons from a crotchety old miser so unpleasant that dogs run from him on sight? That even the hungriest beggars place him on their no-try list? That the bitterest weather can't equal him in terms of icy temperament?

Let's find out.

This is the third book in Thomas Nelson's *52 Little Lessons* series. It differs from the previous two because of its main character's shortcomings. Ebenezer Scrooge is so strikingly selfish that he inspired a noun that now appears in *Merriam-Webster's Dictionary*: *"Scrooge: a miserly person. Her father is a real scrooge and refuses to pay her way through college, even though he can easily afford it."*

On the other hand, George Bailey and Jean Valjean—the respective main characters in *52 Little Lessons from It's a Wonderful Life* and *52 Little Lessons from Les Misérables*—are honorable men throughout most of their stories. Perfect? No. Both men learn significant life lessons: Bailey late in his story, Valjean early in his. But both bring out the best in the people around them. Both put others above self. Both inspire us.

In *A Christmas Carol* by Charles Dickens, however, Ebenezer Scrooge is everything George Bailey and Jean Valjean are not: he's wealthy, selfish, and utterly discontent. A man not revered but despised. A man nobody wants to be like. And because Scrooge's redemption doesn't come until the end of the story, Dickens's portrayal of him is like describing a train wreck in great detail before exalting the fancy caboose at the end.

All of which is to say that *52 Little Lessons from A Christmas Carol* is tinted with a fair share of how-*not*-to-live lessons as well as how-to-live lessons. We learn from both. Scripture is filled with both. We read about the good Samaritan helping a man who's been beaten in order to learn from someone who does the right thing. We read about a Pharisee who lauds his self-perceived righteousness and snubs a lowly tax collector in order to learn from someone who does the wrong thing.

Dickens understands this, for he wrote a story that reaches us from both perspectives and is leavened with the author's faith. "My study of Dickens has convinced me that he was a Christian and that he wrote unapologetically as a Christian," writes Gary L. Colledge in *God and Charles Dickens*. "Dickens's Christian faith and Christian worldview undergirded all that he wrote."

Beyond writing a book especially for his children called *The Life of Our Lord,* Dickens, in a speech at a children's hospital, called Christ "the universal embodiment of all mercy and compassion, Him who once was a child himself, and a poor one."

But the author's Christianity is not the stuff of rules and regulations and doctrine; no scene in the book takes place in a church or involves the clergy. His Christianity is about the simple, and excruciatingly difficult, task of living out the example of Jesus in our everyday lives. To Dickens, writes Colledge, "religion suggested false piety and paraded spirituality." The church was to be "the guardian and facilitator" of "service to others"—but it was not living up to that ideal.

As such, just as the Pharisees were wary of Jesus, so was the church wary of Dickens. Rev. David Macrae scolded him in a letter, saying his books—including such notables as *Great Expectations* and *A Tale of Two Cities*—lacked positive portrayal of Christian characters. He was, some argued, far too simple. Too nuts-and-bolts. Too passionate about the ragamuffin Jesus than about the hierarchy of the, *ahem*, Church of England.

Dickens wanted nothing to do with the church's standards, replying to Macrae that when writing his books, "one of my most constant and most earnest endeavours has been to exhibit in all my good people some faint reflections of the teachings of our great Master, and . . . to lead the reader up to those teachings as the great source of all moral goodness."

A Christmas Carol—Dickens's "charity sermon," writes Michael Hearn in *The Annotated Christmas Carol*—"was preached not in the pulpit at Westminster, but by the hearth of the common man. . . . There are biblical references here and there, but what Dickens emphasized were the good works of Christ."

"If ever there was a message full of what modern people call true Christianity, the direct appeal to the common heart, a faith that was simple, a hope that was infinite, and a charity that was omnivorous, if ever there came among men what they call the Christianity of Christ, it was in the message of Dickens," writes G. K. Chesterton.

* * *

A Christmas Carol was published in 1843. Dickens, only thirty-one at the time, wrote the Victorian-era novella in a scant six weeks. It was the smallest of his cadre of books, many of which wound up in the eight-hundred-page range. At sixty-six pages, it is a mere 5 percent of Victor Hugo's 1,463-page *Les Misérables*, though it proved to be Dickens's most popular book. And it still sells briskly more than a century and a half later.

Indeed, the book further established Dickens as the world's most popular author of his time. In England, he was revered. When coming to America, his arrival was the nineteenth-century equivalent of the Beatles' crossing the pond for *The Ed Sullivan Show* in 1964. He was mobbed by fans wherever he went and sometimes signed up to five hundred autographs at a time.

You wouldn't think of disrespecting such musicians by tampering with their music, right? Thus, I will leave Dickens's British spellings just as he intended them. Expect to see a *u* here or there where you normally don't.

As for the Ghosts that come to enlighten Scrooge, even if the movie versions have depicted them as male or female, Dickens referred to them without gender, so they will be "its" in this book.

The story, of course, has been translated in an array of ways—movies, theater, and opera among them. For the most part, I base my analysis on Dickens's novella. However, because other interpretations of a story can bring deeper meaning, I occasionally refer to various movie versions as well.

Most of you know the basic framing of the story, but you may not be as familiar with the nuances within. "It's like *Hamlet*," said Patrick Stewart, who played a classic Scrooge in a Broadway production of the story. "Half the world knows, 'To be, or not to be,' but very little else. Everybody knows 'Bah, humbug!' but not the real *Carol*."

I hope by book's end you'll know the story better and realize that Scrooge does have something in common with George Bailey and Jean Valjean: with help from others, he is enlightened to become a better man than he was. What's more, I hope you'll know *yourself* better. I certainly gained perspective on myself from researching and writing it, not that I'm particularly proud of all I discovered.

But perspective on ourselves is critical. It's easy for believers to see themselves as Peter during his bold confession of Christ, but not as Peter when he cowardly denied Christ. Likewise, it will be easier to see ourselves as, say, Bob Cratchit or the kindhearted nephew, Fred, in *A Christmas Carol* than as Scrooge. We like to think the best of ourselves.

But doesn't Scripture suggest we all have a touch of Scrooge in us (Romans 3:23)? And can't we all benefit from reexamining who we've become in our own life stories?

In Bob Cratchit, Fred, and others, we'll see honorable examples of human behavior—and I'll discuss such. But *A Christmas Carol* is largely a book about a man not nearly so honorable and who thus can't help but be shrouded in dark shades of regret. As such, my analysis of the story won't provide the instant illumination of a switched-on floodlight but, I hope, the gradual lighting of a roomful of candles glowing after one match strike at a time.

Regardless of where you might be on your spiritual journey, my hope is that *52 Little Lessons from A Christmas Carol* brings you a little more light.

LESSON 1

Context Clarifies a Story

*There is no doubt that Marley was dead. This must
be distinctly understood, or nothing wonderful
can come of the story I am going to relate.*
—THE BOOK'S NARRATOR, ON THE OPENING PAGE

Of all Charles Dickens's books, *A Christmas Carol* is his most popular, and—though highbrow critics might disagree—some believe his best. Given its popularity, given that everybody from George C. Scott to The Muppets has starred in one of the more than twenty film versions of it, and given that "Scrooge" and "Bah humbug!" have become staples of the English language, I assume most of you, dear readers, are familiar with the story at some level.

If so, may the Ghost of Reading Future transport you directly to lesson 2. For those who are unfamiliar with the plot or need a refresher course, here's a version that you can read faster than the pre-Ghost Scrooge could scare off a Christmas caroler.

Ebenezer Scrooge sits in his drafty office being mean to people who love Christmas, including his clerk, Bob Cratchit; his nephew, Fred; and two solicitors who stop to seek donations for the poor and leave with nothing but a rebuke.

That night, Christmas Eve, Scrooge is visited by the Ghost of his former partner, Jacob Marley, who died seven years earlier. Like Scrooge, Marley was a greedy old coot. The chain-dragging Ghost of Marley tells Scrooge that he'll be visited by three other Ghosts in the wee hours in an attempt to help him avoid the shackles that weigh down Marley. Scrooge goes to bed wondering if he's just had some bad food for dinner.

The Ghost of Christmas Past arrives and whisks him back to memories of a kinder, gentler, young Scrooge. Scrooge sees his lonely childhood; the boarding school he attended; Fan, his now-deceased, beloved sister; a festive Christmas party thrown by his old boss, Mr. Fezziwig; and his heartthrob, Belle, whom he gave up to follow the money. Belle wound up with a family of her own, her joy racking Scrooge with regret. "Enough!" he says, in essence. "Show over. Get me back to my regularly scheduled so-called life."

Enter the Ghost of Christmas Present, who shows Scrooge scenes of Christmas joy among the poor and blue-collar crowd. Scrooge and the Spirit visit the home of Bob Cratchit. Bob's young son, Tiny Tim, is ill, Scrooge observes. "I see an empty chair," the Spirit says, "where Tiny Tim once sat." The Spirit and Scrooge visit holiday celebrations at a miners' cottage, at a lighthouse, and on a ship. Then he gives Scrooge a peek at his nephew's Christmas gathering, where Fred speaks of his uncle not with the disdain others do, but with pity. Finally, Scrooge is introduced to two emaciated children, Ignorance and Want, symbols of society's neglect of the poor. "Beware of these two," the Spirit warns. When Scrooge shows concern for their welfare, the Ghost heaps guilt on Scrooge by rattling off a statement he'd made when the two solicitors had come to his office seeking money for the poor: "Are there no prisons? Are there no workhouses?"

The third Spirit, the Ghost of Christmas Yet to Come, shows Scrooge Christmas Day a year from now. Tiny Tim is dead; with his meager salary, Cratchit apparently couldn't get the boy the care he needed. The Spirit shows Scrooge the aftermath of a "wretched man's" death: businessmen will attend the service only if lunch is served, and three people, including the undertaker, steal the man's possessions while the corpse lies in bed. Finally, the Spirit shows Ebenezer the dead man's tombstone. Surprise, surprise—it's Scrooge!

Sobbing, Scrooge vows to change his ways. And does. He awakens the next morning with a renewed spirit. He asks a young boy outside what day it is, and the reply is one of the greatest moments of the book: "To-day! Why, Christmas Day." Scrooge is giddy. Smiling. Laughing. He orders the largest turkey in town for Bob Cratchit's family. He visits his nephew, Fred, who's stunned and thrilled to see him.

The following day Scrooge gives Cratchit a raise and becomes like a "second father" to Tiny Tim. Scrooge emerges as Mr. Christmas. And Dickens closes the story with five words from the little tyke himself: "God bless us every one."

A Christmas Carol is, to some, a ghost story, to others a Christmas fantasy with a comedic twist. Some see it as a time-travel narrative, others as biting social commentary on how the rich look down on the poor. It's actually all four.

And more.

When you think of *A Christmas Carol*, what comes to mind? The book or one of its many film adaptations? What is your favorite part of the story and why?

_____

_____

_____

_____

A perennial holiday favorite, Dickens's novel is nearly 180 years old. What do you think are the reasons for its longevity?

_____

_____

_____

Growing Wiser Means Getting Uncomfortable

May it haunt [the reader's house] pleasantly.
—FROM THE PREFACE TO *A CHRISTMAS CAROL*

Charles Dickens did not write *A Christmas Carol* simply to entertain us as readers, even if he succeeded grandly in doing so. Beyond entertaining us, Dickens wanted to make us *uncomfortable,* because it's only after we get a touch uneasy with ourselves that we open ourselves to change.

Oh, sure, you can defend the book as a social and political commentary wherein the author's target is a coldhearted British government that neglects the poor—worse, discriminates against them, middle-class property owners not even allowed to vote until the passage of the Great Reform Act in 1832. Certainly Dickens wanted to rally the public to action regarding the poor; he had known the pangs of poverty himself as a child and, in books such as *Nicholas Nickleby* and *Oliver Twist*, exudes a deep sensitivity to the less fortunate.

That said, he wanted us individual readers to squirm a bit when we contrast our lives with a higher standard. "I have always striven in my writings, to express veneration for the life and lessons of my Savior," Dickens said. And one of those lessons is to love others as Jesus loved us—no small challenge.

Even if Dickens's intent was aimed at government reform, doesn't that begin with individual reform? "Everybody thinks of changing humanity," writes author Leo Tolstoy, "but nobody thinks of changing himself."

Dickens wants us, as individuals, to confront our own Ghosts. He wants us to feel the chill of regret if necessary and, like Scrooge, to make changes in how we live. All, of course, while maintaining proper Dickens Christmas cheer, with a bounty of food. And with a subtle but unmistakable seasoning of humor.

"I have endeavoured in this Ghostly little book, to raise the Ghost of an Idea, which shall not put my readers out of humour with themselves, with each other, with the season, or with me," reads his preface. "May it haunt their houses pleasantly, and no one wish to lay it."

Dickens is no spoilsport who has come to rain on our Christmas parades. He's more like a good-hearted, well-humored pastor who wants to tickle our funny bones while, at the same time, challenging our souls. (Though he might chafe at the pastor metaphor; Dickens is all about street-level spirituality, unencumbered by people in authority.)

As the story unfolds, it's obvious that Dickens has sprinkled it with humor as a means to an end: to force us, as he forced Scrooge, to confront any rattling chains we might have in our life closets.

His prelude suggests he wants—dare we say, has *great expectations* for—his story to marinate in our souls long after we've read it. He wants not only to entertain but to teach. He wants to offer not only a story but also a sermon: a fanciful moral wrapped in dark paper but crowned with a festive Christmas bow.

The word *haunt*, taken literally, may connote physical ghosts. But *haunt* also means "to visit frequently," "to have a disquieting or harmful effect on," "to reappear continually in." In other words, the story sticks with us after we're through reading it. And it disquiets us in the best of ways, much as the Holy Spirit disquiets us when it's necessary for us to make changes in our lives.

"*A Christmas Carol* is designed not to make us think or see or know, but to make us feel," writes Norrie Epstein in *The Friendly Dickens*. "For Dickens, the power of the imagination expressed through fiction is like the Ghosts, an agent of regeneration."

I suggest that this design to feel is not to produce some temporary emotional high, but to create a spark that might lead to flames of action: changing how we look at the world, changing how we act in the world, and ultimately changing how we will be remembered in the world. In short, Dickens is shooting for nothing less than spiritual or moral revival in those of us who read his story.

Robert Louis Stevenson was so inspired by *A Christmas Carol* and a second Dickens Christmas offering, *The Chimes*, that he wrote, "I have cried my eyes out. I want to go out and comfort someone—I *shall* give money."

Isaac Newton's first law of motion suggests that everything continues in a state of rest unless it is compelled to change by forces impressed upon it. *A Christmas Carol* is just such a force, gently impressed upon us as if the author is saying, "Get up off that couch that I might politely bother you."

I say as much to the university journalism students I teach: if they're not feeling uncomfortable from time to time, they're not growing as journalists. Just as resistance against something is the basis for making an athlete better—lifting weights, swimming in a pool, running up a hill—so can literature make us uncomfortable . . . and better.

Dickens's idea was that readers should be transformed into the image of the One whose inspiration was foundational to his life and to his stories. Second Corinthians 3:18 talks of "being transformed into his image with ever-increasing glory."

Isn't that what happens to Scrooge? And shouldn't that be what's happening to us as we hone our lives for God's glory? If so, let us, with good Christmas cheer, get on with learning the story at a deeper level. Let's get on with understanding what life lessons *A Christmas Carol* might offer and get on with this business of being "pleasantly haunted."

The word *haunt* doesn't have to mean something scary. It can mean "to visit frequently." Who are the people (and places) that leave your heart "pleasantly haunted"? Take a brief moment to thank God for placing them in your life.

_____

_____

_____

_____

Discomfort often leads to wisdom. Think of a time in your life when you had to undergo something painful or uncomfortable. How were you wiser or more mature afterward?

_____

_____

_____

LESSON 3

It's Not About You

Solitary as an oyster.
—The narrator, on Scrooge

Ebenezer Scrooge proudly wears his distaste for anything beyond money like a suit of armor. We aren't privy to his innermost thoughts or fears, but outwardly, he seems perfectly content in his total discontentedness, happily unhappy that the only one who matters on this earth is named Ebenezer Scrooge.

He lives his life in a rut well-rusted by time, bitterness, and regret, like a shipwreck encrusted with barnacles that have clung to it so stubbornly long that they have become part of the vessel itself.

Then comes that wild and crazy Christmas Eve/Christmas

morning when Jacob Marley and the three Spirits—sounds like some sixties rock band—expose him for the lonely, needy, desperate man he really is.

Until then, Scrooge is the poster boy for unhappy people who grumble their way through life, believing that they benefit by walling themselves off from others. That it *is* all about them.

Dickens, of course, sees Scrooge for who he really is: a dead man walking. He is cold. He is tight-fisted. He is "self-contained." In the opening stave, or chapter—literally, a stanza in a poem or song—we learn Scrooge has never bothered to paint out the name of his long-dead partner, Marley, on the sign of his business's door and is known to answer to Scrooge or Marley. "It was all the same to him," writes the narrator.

The subtle message: Though obviously redeemable—that, after all, is the point of the book—Scrooge is Marley without the physical chains. He's impervious to weather: "no warmth could warm, nor wintry weather chill him." He's impervious to feelings: "solitary as an oyster." He's impervious to people. And he is named, apparently, from the slang word *scrooge*: to crowd or squeeze, the star of our show being "a squeezing, wrenching, grasping, scraping, clutching, covetous old sinner!"

Nobody dares to greet him on the street. Beggars ignore him. Children fear him. Even dogs sense he's bad news. "When they saw him coming, [dogs] would tug their owners into doorways and up courts," the narrator tells us.

Scrooge, meanwhile, is seemingly content that others return his coldness with a coldness of their own. "What did Scrooge care?" writes the narrator. "It was the very thing he liked. To edge his way along the crowded paths of life, warning all human sympathy to keep its distance."

He obsesses with the trivial—the cost of a chunk or two of coal to bring warmth to his office and to his employee, Bob Cratchit—and ignores the profound: People. God. The suffering and joy of others.

"Man's sensitivity to little things and insensitivity to the greatest things are marks of a strange disorder," writes Blaise Pascal, the seventeenth-century French religious philosopher.

So what are the "greatest things"? When a Pharisee asks Jesus that question—specifically, what are the most important commandments?—Jesus doesn't roll out a list of dos and don'ts. Instead, he says, with a touch of my paraphrasing: "You want to know what's important? Relationships. With God. And with people." Specifically: "'Love the Lord your God with all your heart and with all your soul and with all your mind.' This is the first and greatest commandment. And the second is like it: 'Love your neighbor as yourself'" (Matthew 22:37–39).

Why doesn't Scrooge see this? Because ignorance is bliss, or so he thinks. The first step in making a life change is awareness. "The fear of the LORD is the beginning of knowledge," says Proverbs 1:7, "but fools despise wisdom and instruction." Thus, if we remain unaware of our deficiencies, if we dare not look in the mirror, if we busy ourselves with Pascal's "little things," then we never have to come face-to-face with our true fear: the real *us*.

The irony, of course, is that until we do so, it doesn't matter who we pretend is staring back at us in that mirror. As long as we think life is about only *that* person and nobody else, we're destined to slowly suffocate in worship of self. So day after day, we, like Scrooge, keep pretending we're fully alive when, in fact, we may only be breathing.

Dickens describes Ebenezer Scrooge as "solitary as an oyster." Considering that not-so-appealing oysters can be the source of something exquisite—pearls—how did Scrooge's frightening experience bring about something unexpected and beautiful?

_____

_____

_____

_____

Read Proverbs 1:7. Why does turning our backs on wisdom and instruction make us foolish? Did you ever make this choice in your own life? What did you learn?

_____

_____

_____

LESSON 4

Misery Loves Company

Can you? Can you sit down?
—Scrooge, to the Ghost of Jacob Marley

As the story begins, Scrooge encounters four men—Cratchit, Fred, and two alms-for-the-poor solicitors—and he dismisses them with an iciness as brittle as the Christmas Eve weather outside.

Why? Because each reminds Scrooge of what he is *not*, leaving him two options: to face his deficiencies and do something about them, or to rationalize that the problem couldn't possibly be *him* so it must be *them*. These others include Fred, his insufferably upbeat nephew who wears his Christmas Spirit loud and proud; the two men raising money for the poor with far too much compassion for Scrooge's taste; and Cratchit, Scrooge's clerk, who bothers his boss because he wants to take off Christmas Day. Grumbles Scrooge, "I pay a day's wages for no work."

What Scrooge is really saying is this: *If I'm going to be miserable, then I want the people around me to be just as miserable. No, make that more miserable.*

It's a wonder discontent people such as Scrooge hire such content people as Cratchit, because it places them in an uncomfortable position. It constantly reminds them of their own discontentedness. Virtue is a light that frightens those who live in darkness.

I remember the moment I first realized as much. I think of it as my light-on-the-cockroach moment. I was a sophomore in high school, a time when belonging was important and our safe haven was cliques. My jock-oriented circle was having a party at the house of a friend whose parents were out of town for the weekend. We purposely didn't tell one particular person about it because, well, he wasn't deemed cool enough.

But like the rest of us, he desperately wanted to belong. Midway through the party someone glanced out the window and saw him walking up to the door. "Quick, hide!" someone said. And we did. Behind furniture. In the garage. Out back. When nobody answered the door, the uninvited guest looked through the window and saw dozens of us hiding behind furniture like cockroaches that had suddenly seen the light and scurried for the dark.

It was the first time in my life I realized that I didn't particularly like the person looking back at me in the mirror. I saw self-righteousness. Snobbery. Hypocrisy. It was the beginning of a major life change for me. If Scrooge's turnaround was triggered by the Ghost of his old business partner and three Spirits, mine was triggered by an uninvited guest to a party. The turnaround was then imbued by the grace of God, who I soon came to realize was not some celestial cop or grim-faced reaper, but the Creator of the universe, the Maker of me, and the Redeemer of all, including selfish punks like me.

We either conform to the world or to the One who made the world. As Bob Dylan sings: "It may be the devil or it may be the Lord / But you're gonna have to serve somebody."

Scrooge serves himself. And when encountering those who serve more admirably, he mindlessly dismisses them as people who are exploiting him (Cratchit), needling him with run-amuck Christmas Spirit (Fred), or guilting him into giving to the poor (the two collecting donations for the down-and-out). "Are there no prisons?" asks Scrooge. "And the Union workhouses?"

The more he grumbles, the more Scrooge convinces himself that he is a victim to all this blather. The more he feels like a victim, the less responsibility he feels to change. And the less responsibility he feels to change, the more he becomes encrusted in his own meaninglessness.

As a speaker, one of the first lessons you learn is that an energy-deficient audience will either bring you down to its level or you will bring it up to yours. Scrooge, in his skewed vision, is a defiant audience of one refusing to rise above his own misery. He will immerse himself in his personal anguish, and he will do all in his power to see that others are as unhappy as he.

Ah, but the Powers That Be have different plans for Mr. Scrooge.

Why does pessimism often attract more company than optimism? How does sharing our misery with others prevent us from making needed changes in our lives?

_____

_____

_____

_____

Have you ever excluded or looked down on someone for not fitting in or being part of your circle of friends? How does it make you feel in retrospect? What does Scripture reveal about this?

_____

_____

_____

LESSON 5

Don't Let People Steal Your Joy

I'll keep Christmas humour to the last.
So a Merry Christmas, uncle!
—Scrooge's nephew, Fred, after their spirited debate

To see how Fred, Bob, and the two solicitors react to Scrooge's curmudgeonly humbugging is to appreciate a lesson in contentedness. None of the men allows Scrooge's dark perspective to dim his own optimism about life. The four don't lower their standards to his.

Take Fred. "A merry Christmas, uncle!" he greets Scrooge upon entering the man's place of business. "God save you!"

"Bah, humbug!" says Scrooge.

Fred, the narrator tells us, is "in a glow." His eyes sparkle. He's so full of peace and goodwill toward men that they gush out of him with all the energy of a high-mountain waterfall. And it irks Scrooge, who attempts to convince his nephew that only fools believe in all this Christmas Spirit stuff.

Fred defends such spirit with gusto, with reason, and with pride, but he never lets that become more important than what really matters to him in this scenario: his uncle. He refuses to take personally Scrooge's harsh retorts, even after the older man says, "If I could work my will, every idiot who goes about with 'Merry Christmas,' on his lips, should be boiled with his own pudding, and buried with a stake of holly through his heart."

In England at mid-nineteenth century, Christmas spirit had fizzled across the land, the victim of long Puritan rule that, as far back as 1652, had demanded that "no observance shall be had of the five and twentieth of December, commonly called Christmas day." The Industrial Revolution had further dampened the celebration by insisting that factories keep running on Christmas Day.

Dickens railed against such a heartless approach to the season. Remembered Dickens's daughter, Mamie, after her father had died, "Christmas was always a time which in our home was looked forward to with eagerness and delight, and to my father it was a time dearer than any other part of the year, I think. He loved Christmas for its deep significance as well as for its joys."

Fred—patterned after Dickens, said friends of the author— responds to Scrooge by saying Christmas has made him a better person. Scrooge belittles him with sarcasm. Say what you will about the old man, but he does have a wry, if subtle, sense of humor. "You're quite a powerful speaker, sir. I wonder you don't go into Parliament."

Fred responds by inviting Scrooge for dinner with his wife and friends, which shifts Scrooge's anti-Christmas stance to an anti-love-in-general stance. Fred persists. Scrooge resists and invites the young man to leave—repeatedly. And leave he does, but, writes the narrator, "without an angry word," stopping to wish Cratchit a Merry Christmas on his way out.

We live in a world that has the potential to suck the joy right out of us. Like Scrooge, it can be a world that mocks us, demeans us, and tugs at us to drop a sunny disposition and to become morbid and cynical like so many others. But we would do well to, like Fred, stay steadfast in our passion to "not be overcome by evil, but overcome evil with good" (Romans 12:21).

The two solicitors for the poor—next on Scrooge's be-nasty-to list—could have stooped to Ebenezer's bitterness. In his response to their request Scrooge suggests the poor deserve their plight. They are, Scrooge says, "surplus population."

While the two men defend the poor, they do not criticize Scrooge for his insensitivity to the plight of those in need. Instead, they take Scrooge's hint—"Good afternoon, gentlemen!"—and leave.

He then turns his temper on Cratchit, fueled by an intervening episode of someone foisting more ghastly Christmas Spirit on him: a young boy who dares sing "God bless you merry gentleman!" at the front door of the business. Scrooge threatens the boy with a ruler, then turns on Cratchit for wanting Christmas Day off.

Scrooge uses a common passive-aggressive ploy of playing the part of victim: the numb-fingered Cratchit—he's heating his hands by a candle—can have the day off, sure, but only if he's made to feel duly guilty for "picking a man's pocket" by expecting a full day's pay for no work.

Does Scrooge dampen Cratchit's Christmas Spirit? No. On his way home from work, the clerk happily slides on the snow with the neighborhood boys—"No less than twenty times!"—and runs home to play a Christmas Eve game of blindman's buff with his children.

The world is full of Scrooge-like people who want us to join them in their misery. Our job is not to join them but to love them. Respect them. Encourage them to climb out of whatever dark hole they've found comfort in. Then we wrap up for the cold and slide through that Christmas Eve snow as if we were forever young.

Fred and Cratchit's joy prevents Scrooge's harsh retorts from getting under their skin. Do you know someone who is perpetually negative? What tools has God given you to deal with their pessimistic outlook?

_____

_____

_____

_____

Have you ever had one of those days where the world's cynicism seems to rub off on you? Look up *joy* in a Bible concordance or online search engine. List here your favorite verses about joy to encourage your spirit this week.

_____

_____

_____

LESSON 6

It's About More Than Christmas

The only time I know of, in the long calendar
of the year, when men and women seem by one
consent to open their shut-up hearts freely.
—Scrooge's nephew, Fred

When you think about it, it's odd that the world selects a particular time of year when everyone is supposed to be nice to everyone else. The unspoken inference is that you should feel no particular responsibility toward others the rest of the year. Oh, sure, children might be told their Christmas cache is dependent on whether they've been naughty or nice all year long, but the overriding message is that this is a special season of kindness.

Dickens was particularly fond of the Christmas season, and he expresses that fondness in *A Christmas Carol* through Bob and Fred, the latter of whom makes an impassioned defense of Christmas: "a kind, forgiving, charitable, pleasant time: the only time I know of, in the long calendar of the year, when men and women seem by one consent to open their hearts freely."

Hear! Hear! But shouldn't we amortize such spirit all year long instead of offering only a lump-sum payment come December? The point isn't to deride such others-oriented thinking, but to remind us all that that's how Scripture suggests we should live: all year long, 24/7. Every day. In good times and in bad times. In sickness and in health. Joyfully. With others in mind. "Do nothing out of selfish ambition or vain conceit," says Philippians 2:3. "Rather, in humility value others above yourselves." At Christmastime. And *not* at Christmastime. All the time.

Many people share Fred's giddiness over Christmas; the holiday *does* seem to bring out the best in us. But it does so because it encourages us to be who God intends for us to be all the time: people of peace and goodwill toward others. So the season emerges as a prototype of idealism—the way life should *always* be, not just when the malls erect their Christmas displays every November. (Okay, October. Well, okay, in some cases, September.)

Likewise, for Dickens, Christmas becomes a metaphor for life itself, the unwritten suggestion that in keeping Christmas, we are, in essence, keeping *Christ*—the one on whom the celebration rests. The one whom Tiny Tim will remind us "made lame beggars walk and blind men see." The one who is the quiet inspiration for the changes that will come to Scrooge.

When Fred exalts Christmas—"I believe that it *has* done me good, and *will* do me good; and I say, God bless it!"—he's really exalting the Author of such joy. He's exalting the idea that others-oriented joy should be more than temporary ceasefire from the normality of a self-oriented, humdrum life but should represent life at its fullest—all the time.

Stanley Weintraub's book *Silent Night* (Plume, 2002) tells of a real-life cease-fire. In 1914, World War I soldiers who were fighting each other laid down their arms and joined in spontaneous celebration. The catalyst for this unofficial truce? Christmas Eve. They climbed out of the trenches to sing carols, exchange gifts, and even play soccer. The next day, they went about the task at hand: trying to kill each other.

Writes Weintraub, "Like a dream, when it was over, men wondered at it, then went on with the grim business at hand. Under the rigid discipline of wartime command authority, that business was killing."

The ability to stop fighting and to treat one another civilly offers an ironic lesson amid war: *Peace is attainable. We needn't hate one another. We can stop fighting if we agree to.* Yet just as the soldiers returned to war after a short respite, we too often do the same after Christmas: we return from temporarily caring for others to warring with them.

Why not just call a truce for good, and, even without the holly and ivy, spread the cheer throughout the year?

The author refers to Christmas as "a prototype of idealism, the way life should *always* be." What are some creative, meaningful ways to spread the joy of Christmastime throughout the year?

_____

_____

_____

_____

This chapter recounts the story of a remarkable cease-fire moment from World War I. This week, whom can you "climb out of the trenches for" and share the love of Christ with? What does that sharing look like?

_____

_____

_____

See Life as a Child

*The office was closed in a twinkling, and
[Cratchit], with the long ends of his white comforter
dangling below his waist . . . went down a slide
on Cornhill, at the end of a lane of boys, twenty
times in honour of its being Christmas-eve.*
—The narrator, on Cratchit's Christmas
Eve walk home from work

Earlier we touched on Bob Cratchit's reaction to Scrooge's grumpiness. On his way home from work after he'd been scolded by Scrooge for wanting a day off, Cratchit joins some local boys for some "snow sliding." Then, once home, he joins his children to play a game of blindman's buff. In other words, Cratchit becomes like a child.

At first glance, Cratchit's becoming childlike in the aftermath of Scrooge's huffing and puffing might seem insignificant, a minor detail amid Dickens's major theme. But it isn't minor at all. In fact, as the story unfolds, we'll see that part of what Scrooge has lost is the very thing Cratchit still possesses: the ability to see life through the eyes of a child.

The narrator suggests there's value in looking at the world from a child's perspective. Scrooge is a man of wealth and position, a man who employs others, a man to whom solicitors come seeking help. In other words, he is an important *adult*. Yet the narrator points out it's the children, not Scrooge, who *get it*. They are living life to its fullest. They live with zest as flush as their rosy cheeks.

This is interesting when you consider that scene in the gospel of Matthew when the disciples rebuked those who brought little children to Jesus. Jesus could have said, "Children are insignificant. It's the adults who have their acts together. Keep the little critters away." Instead, he said, "Let the little children come to me, and do not hinder them, for the kingdom of heaven belongs to such as these" (Matthew 19:14).

Jesus saw something special in children. Could it be that they are not jaded by the sophistication of the world? That they are exuberant about life? Humble? Willing to admit their needs? Willing to trust that others can help them? Unpretentious? Adventurous? Lighthearted? Imaginative?

In short, could it be that children are everything the Scrooges of the world are not? Scrooge, as we'll see in more depth later, was once such a child but lost that zeal along life's way. He is jaded. Pretentious. Proud. Time has eroded whatever innocence he once had and has left him a joyless soul.

When the narrator describes Cratchit sliding on the snow with the local boys, the visual image is a delightful contrast. He's not properly dressed for such sport—he is, after all, an adult on his way home from work, and sliding is for kids—but the narrator clearly endorses his throw-caution-to-the-wind decision.

And where can we surmise that Scrooge's life of promise turned toward dark and selfish ways? "Scrooge's failure as a human being," writes Michael Hearn, author of *The Annotated Christmas Carol* (Norton, 1976), "began early, in suppressing the kindly sentiments of his childhood."

"If we can only preserve ourselves from growing up," Dickens wrote in "When We Stopped Growing" (*Household Words*, January 1, 1853), "we shall never grow old, and the young may love us to the last. Not to be too wise, not to be too stately, not to be too rough with innocent fancies, or to treat them with too much lightness . . . are points to be remembered that may do us all good in our years to come."

"It is good to be children sometimes," Dickens writes, as the narrator in *Carol*, "and never better than at Christmas, when its mighty Founder was a child himself."

We shouldn't underestimate the power of children as examples in our lives. "Truly I tell you, unless you change and become like little children, you will never enter the kingdom of heaven," Jesus said in Matthew 18:3.

That is high praise for the mindsets of the young—and, at first blush, some might slough off such thinking as, well, child's play. But remember the context here: Jesus was exalting children regarding access to eternal life. Trivial? Not at all. The inference? *The kids are onto something here. Pay attention. Sometimes it's the stuff that we don't think is profound that is utterly profound.* Or, as 1 Corinthians 1:27 says, "God chose the foolish things of the world to shame the wise; God chose the weak things of the world to shame the strong."

In a Ghost of Christmas Yet to Come scene, young Peter Cratchit reads Mark 9:36 to his mother and siblings: "And he took a child, and set him in the midst of them" (KJV).

After all, where, ultimately, will Scrooge find his redemption? In a little boy—Tiny Tim.

Writes the narrator, who injects an occasional opinion: "I should have liked, I do confess, to have had the lightest license of a child and yet been man enough to know its value."

See Life as a Child

The Christmas season is an ideal time to celebrate the innocence
and unbridled joy of children. How does seeing life as a child help
us experience and cope with our daily struggles from a different
perspective?

_____

_____

_____

_____

What are some ways you can play this week—with your own
children or as a child—that can help open you up to Jesus'
encouragement in Matthew 18:3?

_____

_____

_____

LESSON 8

Everyone Has Value

*If they would rather die, they had better do
it, and decrease the surplus population.*
—SCROOGE, TO THE TWO MEN SEEKING CONTRIBUTIONS
FOR THE POOR, AFTER ONE MENTIONS THAT SOME
LIVING IN POVERTY WOULD RATHER DIE THAN LIVE
IN THE SQUALID CONDITIONS OF A WORKHOUSE

Scrooge is both comical and caustic at the same time. Fred laughs
off his uncle's curmudgeonly ways, but when the two solicitors drop
by to raise money for the poor, Scrooge's countenance plunges from
"Ebenezer just being Ebenezer" to Ebenezer being shockingly cold
toward his fellow man. The poor, he suggests, are only taking up

space; it might be better if they were to die and leave more space for the rest of us.

In many ways, Dickens's book is a thumbing of the nose at British leaders who, at the time, would punish down-on-their-luck people for their poverty. Some elitists wondered if the poor even deserved to live; among them was economist Thomas Robert Malthus, whose views disgusted Dickens. Malthus argued in his *Essay on the Principle of Population* (1798) that population growth would always outpace food supply, resulting in unavoidable poverty and starvation. In his pamphlet "The Crisis," Malthus argued that any man unable to sustain himself had no right to live, period.

Dickens's concern for the poor—and, in particular, poor children—was rooted in his own childhood. At age twelve, after his father was sent to debtors' prison, he was forced to work in a blacking factory, putting labels on pots of boot blacking. Two of his siblings died young, not uncommon in nineteenth-century England.

Shortly before writing *A Christmas Carol*, the author toured the Cornish tin mines, where children were forced to work in appallingly severe conditions. After later seeing the suffering of London's half-starved, illiterate street children in government-run workhouses, where conditions were abysmal and those in authority often cruel, he planned to write a pamphlet decrying the government's laws regarding the poor. "The illegality" of such laws, he said, "is quite equal to the inhumanity." Instead of the pamphlet, he chose to write something he thought would have a greater impact: *A Christmas Carol*.

"I have a great faith in the poor," he wrote shortly after the book was published. "I always endeavor to present them in a favourable light to the rich."

Dickens, who wrote a book specifically for his children called *The Life of Our Lord*, believed what Scripture taught: that every human being has value. The psalmist wrote, "For you created my inmost being; you knit me together in my mother's womb. I praise you because I am fearfully and wonderfully made" (Psalm 139:13–14).

Genesis tells of our being created in God's image. In the gospel of Luke, Jesus said, "Be merciful, just as your Father is merciful" (6:36).

Mercy, we shall find, is not Scrooge's strength. Indeed, he is an elitist who finds poor people bothersome, a perspective that wasn't uncommon in the time and place he lived.

A question, however: Will someone's view of mercy, of human dignity, of the value of each life, change when that person suddenly becomes the beneficiary of such mercy himself? Scrooge will soon find out. And he will do so for a reason that might easily be overlooked. The four Ghosts out to redeem him obviously believe he, too, has value.

Otherwise, why would they bother?

Jesus radically upended human interaction when He told us not only to love our neighbors but also our enemies (Matthew 5:43–44). Who are the people in your life whom you consider enemies, or at least someone you would prefer to avoid? What are some ways you can extend an olive branch this week?

_____

_____

_____

_____

Read James 1:27. Why is looking after widows and orphans considered "pure and faultless" religion? How can acknowledging this help you purify your own faith?

_____

_____

_____

Business Isn't Life

*The dealings of my trade were but a drop of water
in the comprehensive ocean of my business!*
—THE GHOST OF JACOB MARLEY, TO SCROOGE

Jacob Marley's Ghost may not have been much to look at. (That handkerchief around its head is how, in those days, the jaws of corpses were tied shut.) The Ghost cries out from time to time. And it "clanks its chains so hideously," suggests the narrator, that it could have been arrested as a public nuisance. But the first Spirit to visit Scrooge is not without insight, among it the notion that business isn't life.

When Marley's Ghost laments "misused opportunities," Scrooge is quick to defend his former partner as a "good man of business."

"Business!" snorts the Ghost. Then it suggests what its real *business* should have been: "Mankind was my business. The common welfare was my business; charity, mercy, forbearance, and benevolence, are, all, my business. The dealings of my trade were but a drop of water in the comprehensive ocean of my business!"

Scrooge, of course, doesn't want to hear this. The Ghost's indictment of Marley is an indictment of Scrooge. The two are like twins; Scrooge even lives in his partner's former house. But the Spirit isn't finished. It goes on to say Christmas is a particularly tough time of year, because the Ghost's selfishness stands out more against the contrast of peace and goodwill.

"Why," asks the Ghost, "did I walk through crowds of fellow-beings with my eyes turned down, and never raise them to that blessed Star which led the Wise Men to a poor abode?"

Enlightening stuff, this. Whatever the Powers That Be at Spirit Camp have been teaching these unearthly disciples, this one is getting it. The Ghost of Marley realizes that Marley had made his life all about work and not about the people around him, nor about the One for whom that blessed star was hung.

It's ironic that to describe Scrooge's fear at hearing this, the narrator says Ebenezer began to "quake" exceedingly. The idea that Scrooge has lived his life for the wrong things is disruptive to Ebenezer. He's not quaking like the "Silent Night" shepherds in reverent fear of a newborn Savior. He's quaking because Marley's Ghost is saying life isn't about the very things the two men built their lives upon: Making money. Work. *Business.*

To a large degree, that's also true in twenty-first-century America. When we meet someone new, what do we first ask? *What do you do?* That's code for "How do you make your money?" As if that were the essence of our lives. Think about it. Nobody asks, "Say, how did you make the world a better place today?" Or "What difference are you making in the lives of those in need?" Or "What do you do to honor God?"

The *Snow White*–inspired bumper sticker we see—"I owe, I owe, so off to work I go!"—explains one reason that work is seen as important. Most people work to provide necessary services to others and money for their families. But that still doesn't explain a culture where workaholism is seen as some sort of badge of honor, where drivers who text think a business deal is more important than another driver's safety, and where many people have far more than they need and yet continue to worship at the idol of business, as did Marley and Scrooge.

I wonder how many people, at the end of their lives, wind up regretting that they lived to work instead of worked to live? As the saying goes, "Nobody, on his deathbed, ever says, 'I wish I'd spent more time at the office.'"

So why, pre-deathbed, do we willingly live the lie?

How does the *business* (or busyness) of life get in the way of the *living* of life?

_____

_____

_____

_____

A strong work ethic is certainly an admirable quality, but how does workaholism prevent us from fulfilling the two greatest commandments to love God and to love our neighbors as ourselves (Matthew 22:36–39)?

_____

_____

_____

You Make the Chains That Shackle You

I wear the chain I forged in life. I made it link by link,
and yard by yard; I girded it on my own free will.
—THE GHOST OF JACOB MARLEY, TO SCROOGE

When Dickens tells us that the Ghost of Jacob Marley is transparent, the author is not speaking metaphorically. You can literally see right through the Ghost. On the other hand, Scrooge is quite the opposite, reacting to the arrival of this unexpected Christmas Eve visitor with doubt, denial, rationalization—just what you'd expect.

Scrooge is not about to reveal his unspoken fear: that he believes this could be the Ghost of his former business partner—a selfish, lonely man quite like Scrooge, the narrator suggests—and that for some reason it has come to confront him. In a wild grasp for some logical explanation, Scrooge opines that it must be something he ate. "You may be an undigested bit of beef, a blot of mustard, a crumb of cheese, a fragment of an underdone potato."

By contrast, the Ghost proves to be not only real but also honest with itself. Most notably, the Ghost takes ownership of the chains that shackle it, chains made of "cash-boxes, keys, padlocks, ledgers, deeds, and heavy purses wrought in steel." In other words, chains made of a life devoted to work and money, the minutia of business, obsessions that choked out any thought about what really matters: relationships.

Say this about Marley's Ghost: it is an enlightened Ghost, seeing clearly the stuff that Marley missed when he was living. The Ghost is contrite, as if it has learned more in death than Marley learned in life. The counting-house, his business, was everything to Marley, and now, the Ghost realizes, it meant nothing. Fool's gold. Marley's business created chains that enslaved him then, though he didn't realize it at the time. And those chains continue to enslave his Ghost now. The Ghost is helpless to free itself from them; it is destined to wander the world and to warn Scrooge and those like him to wake up before it is too late.

What chains in our own lives are shackling us? The first step to any sort of life redirection is awareness, realizing who we are and how we might need to alter our course. Realizing where we are and where we might need to go. Realizing how we've lost our way and how we might find our way home.

Circumstances beyond our control, of course, influence our lives. And it would be insensitive not to acknowledge as much regarding, say, someone who's lost a loved one or been betrayed by a spouse or been in an accident. Yet many people who wallow in discontent do so because of self-inflicted pain. In other words, they create their own chains.

Like Marley and Scrooge, they've built their lives on foundations too fragile to hold them: work, money, fame, achievement, you name it. Or they're wrestling with addictions they won't admit they have. Or they're wallowing in bitterness, unable to let go of a past hurt. The common denominator is they've made choices—in the words of Marley's Ghost, by their "own free will"—that leave them shackled in discontent.

Scrooge fits neatly in that category, even if it has taken the Ghost of his former business partner to offer a wake-up call. And this Ghost is only the opening act for what's to come: three more Ghosts whose penetrating music will shake Scrooge to the core of his soul.

For an apparition, Marley's Ghost is quite self-aware, acknowledging that his eternal chains are self-inflicted, the result of ignoring the truth when he was living. What are some of the chains that shackle you, that prevent you from a deeper relationship with God?

_____

_____

_____

_____

Read Luke 6:46–49. Considering your relationships with friends and loved ones, why is having a strong foundation so important? Who is affected most when our foundation isn't as strong as it needs to be?

_____

_____

_____

Humility Enhances Vision

Scrooge . . . wept to see his poor
forgotten self as he used to be.
—THE NARRATOR, ON SCROOGE'S TRIP BACK
WITH THE GHOST OF CHRISTMAS PAST

The Ghost of Marley may have temporarily gotten Scrooge's attention, but even after being warned that three more Spirits will visit him, Scrooge rationalizes he might have dreamed all this. Then, right on time, the Ghost of Christmas Past whisks apart the curtain of Scrooge's bed. Showtime!

As the Ghost clasps Scrooge's arm and beckons him to rise and walk with it, Ebenezer offers the first hint of humility since Dickens first dipped his pen: "I am a mortal," he says, "and liable to fall."

Whoa! Scrooge admitting he's not invincible? It is the first sign of hope we've seen in the codger: the subtle admission that he's vulnerable and, if not frightened out of his sleeping cap, certainly a bit scared of the unknown.

Ah, but good things happen to people who admit weaknesses. They begin seeing themselves more clearly. More objectively. They begin seeing themselves not so much as *who they would like to be* but *who they are*—for better or worse. And, thus, they are in much better position to become who they would like to be.

It galls me when a celebrity beats up a spouse or significant other or spits out a racial slur or does something else raunchy, then, in the press conference, says, "I apologize. That's not who I am."

Wrong. That may not be *all* of who you are, but it's *part* of who you are—at least for now. And the sooner you own that, the sooner you can get well, can learn a lesson, can put that behind you, and can prove that though it was once who you were, you have changed.

The hardest thing for some people to accept is that they're not who they think they are. Refusing to admit shortcomings short-circuits any hope of getting better. I love this quote from Lieutenant Barral, from *Digressions sur la Navigation du Cap Horn, 1827*: "It is far better to know where one is, and realize that one does not know, than to be certain one is in a place where he is not."

To be certain that you are flawless is a dangerous place to be. You rationalize. Blame others. Make excuses. All this, instead of admitting you're not sure who you are.

Scrooge, to his credit, is starting to see the errors of his ways. When the Ghost of Christmas Past shows its guest the boarding school where Ebenezer once lived, a tear rolls down Scrooge's cheek. When shown a lone child—himself—Scrooge sobs, reminded of the pain he felt as a little boy who was removed from his family. Says the narrator: "[He] wept to see his poor forgotten self as he had used to be." When shown old school friends, the memories bring to Scrooge's voice something "between laughing and crying."

For the first time, Scrooge is dabbling in *awareness* of who he is and who he was, awareness that starts to transition into the next step in personal change: *vision.* "I wish," he says, drying his eyes. "But it's too late now."

When the Spirit asks what he wishes for, Scrooge mentions the little boy who had shown up at his door the previous evening to sing a Christmas carol. "I should like to have given him something: that's all," he tells the Spirit.

The Ghost of Christmas Past has uncorked more emotion in Scrooge than the man might have unleashed in his entire life. He's cried. He's sobbed. He's laughed. He's felt regret. All in a few flashbacks from *This Is Your Life.*

If life change can be looked at as a four-step process—awareness, vision, strategy, and courage—then the old curmudgeon is already three-quarters of the way there. He's embraced awareness (his life has fallen short of what it could have been), caught a vision (perhaps he could be kinder to others), and even imagined a strategy to hatch that vision (he could have given the young Christmas caroler a few shillings)—though the opportunity, he realizes, has passed.

Why this meteoric progress in a man who, the previous afternoon, had been described by the narrator as "hard and sharp as flint"?

Humility, plain and simple. Humility enhances vision. Scrooge drops his shield of arrogance and pride, allowing himself, for the first time, to *see*. To see himself. To see others. To see what was. To see what might be.

In the Bible, the prodigal son goes through a similar process after squandering his wealth and winding up in a pig's sty. Awareness. (*Hm. This isn't working out. My father's servants are eating better than I am.* "He came to his senses," says Luke 15:17.) Vision. (*I need to make a change.*) Strategy. (*I'm going back to Pops and telling him I blew it and I'm not worthy to be his son.*) Courage. (*I'm carrying through with my strategy.*)

What the prodigal son and Scrooge have in common is a realization that the pasts they gave up were pretty good. But it's something they can see only after the scales of pride have fallen from their eyes.

During the visit from the Ghost of Christmas Past, Scrooge begins to reveal the slightest indication of vulnerability. Why does acknowledging painful truths from our past make us so emotional? Is it regret or the opportunity for change that tugs at our heartstrings?

_____

_____

_____

_____

Jesus' compassion and humility provided the blueprint for how we should pattern our faith journey. Why are these two virtues so important in our walk with God?

_____

_____

_____

LESSON 12

To Heal You Must Feel

And he sobbed.
—The narrator, on Scrooge in the
Ghost of Christmas Past moment where
he is alone in the boarding school

Some would call it a chink in his time-rusted armor. The Ghost of Christmas Past brings Scrooge back to the boarding school where he had lived as a boy, and the experience touches Ebenezer deeply.

Touches him. The Spirit's gentle touch, writes the narrator, "appeared still present to the old man's sense of feeling. He was conscious of a thousand odours floating in the air, each one connected with a thousand thoughts, and hopes, and joys, and cares long, long forgotten."

For the first time, Scrooge is reconnected with long-forgotten feelings. What that means is, for the first time, he can get better.

Scrooge is a man with deep hurts, mind you. Presumably, he lost his mother when he was young. His father was cruel; most likely, the man was lost to the boy in many ways. He lost a sister, Fan, who died as a young woman. And he lost Belle, who wanted to spend the rest of her life with him.

And how did he deal with this? By not dealing with it. Instead of dealing with his feelings, he stowed them away in his life's attic and, to forget, busied himself about the business of making money. But that didn't mend his wounds. It only hardened his heart.

In essence, the Spirit takes Scrooge to that attic and says, *You can't move on, you can't get better, and you can't overcome the past until you deal with this stuff.* This is the beginning of Scrooge's metamorphosis into a new man.

In 2012, I had the privilege of going on an Honor Flight trip in which World War II soldiers were flown to Washington, D.C., at no charge and given tours of the memorials that honor them. It was emotional for most of them, but one marine remained stoic as the day unfolded.

Then we arrived at the Iwo Jima Memorial in honor of the U.S. Marine Corps. He took one look at that massive sculpture of the soldiers raising that flag and his head slowly tilted down. His eyes grew misty. And he reached for a handkerchief.

That was stage one of his feel-before-you-heal moment. Stage two came when a Vietnam-era marine saw what was happening and put his arm around the man to support him.

When we feel, we get real with ourselves. When we get real, we humble ourselves. When we humble ourselves, we're open to being helped—by God and by those around us. But we can't be helped unless we welcome that help, which usually means acting on a feeling.

In some Christian circles, feelings are looked upon with suspicion, a straying into the realm of touchy-feely. We are to be faith-and fact-based followers. People of action. And I get that. But we too often fail to acknowledge that which inspires our actions, choices, and tendencies: our feelings. Whenever believers stand in churches and give their testimonies, the catalyst for transformation was daring to feel deeply the pain they were experiencing. And deciding enough was enough.

So that tear on Scrooge's face is no chink in his armor. On the contrary, it's a badge of honor. Light in the darkness.

Do you ever reprimand yourself for being too emotional, too "touchy-feely"? Why should we consider deep feelings to be badges of honor rather than things to be dismissed?

_____

_____

_____

_____

Many of us have a painful past that we are reluctant to revisit. What does Scripture tell us about the heartache we feel? Read Deuteronomy 31:8, Psalm 46:1–3, John 14:26–27, and Philippians 4:6–7 for a good start.

_____

_____

_____

Your Actions Affect Others

*He has the power to render us happy or
unhappy; to make our service light or
burdensome; a pleasure or a toil.*
—Scrooge, to the Ghost of Christmas Past,
about his jovial boss, Mr. Fezziwig

The Ghost of Christmas Past shows Scrooge a Christmas Eve party organized by Ebenezer's first employer, Mr. Fezziwig, when Ebenezer is a young man. "Work can wait," says the boss with giddy anticipation for the fun ahead.

"Shutters up!" he cries with a clap of his hands.

Fezziwig emerges as an engaging host, inviting half the town.

He fills his merchant shop with cake, pies, roasts, and more—and he proceeds, with his affable wife, to outdance everybody there.

It's hard to tell which experience Scrooge finds more fun: watching the party as a young man when it is actually happening or looking back on it as the present-day Scrooge.

That's right, I used *fun* and *Scrooge* in the same sentence, but it is necessary; the narrator describes Scrooge as "out of his wits" with joy. "His heart and soul were in the scene, and with his former self. He . . . enjoyed everything."

The Spirit, perhaps playing devil's advocate to further enlighten his human project, pooh-poohs any praise due Fezziwig for throwing the festive gig. "A small matter," it says, "to make these silly folks so full of gratitude."

When the Ghost of Christmas Past suggests that all Fezziwig has done is use employees' money to put on a party, Scrooge is "heated by the remark," says the narrator, and defends his old boss with gusto. "He has the power to render us happy or unhappy; to make our service light or burdensome; a pleasure or a toil," says Scrooge. "The happiness he gives, is quite as great as if it cost a fortune."

As if Scrooge doesn't stun us enough by crying in the previous scene, he's now asking what price one can put on bringing joy to people. Overnight, he's gone from a selfish boss who hoards coal in his office while his clerk warms his hands over a candle to the Enlightened One, who might as well be channeling theologian and author Frederick Buechner: "If you want to be holy, be kind."

The festive scene prompts Scrooge, as an employer, to contrast Fezziwig's approach to Christmas Eve with his own. The results are convicting. "I should like to be able to say a word or two to my clerk just now!" says Scrooge to the Spirit, obviously feeling shame for treating Cratchit so badly.

The party scene helps Scrooge realize this: we have the ability to make people happy. To make them feel valued. Or, in Scrooge's case, to cause them grief. To make them feel unvalued.

In short, we make a difference in people's lives. And sometimes the biggest difference makers are those who never realize the effect they've had on others.

That lesson was hammered home to me when I had the privilege of writing a book about the first World War II nurse to die after the landings at Normandy. As a girl and young woman, Frances Slanger was essentially told at every turn, *You don't matter.* As a Jewish female growing up in Poland, she was low person on the social ladder. At Ellis Island at age seven, she was detained because of an eye infection though later allowed citizenship. When she expressed interest in being a nurse so she could "serve people less fortunate than I," her parents insisted, "That's not for a Jewish girl." When she persevered and was accepted in nursing school, her supervisors told her she wouldn't make a good nurse. When she persisted and got her degree and voluntarily joined the U.S. Army Nurse Corps, she was initially denied overseas duty because of bad eyesight.

The message: *You're not worthy to make a difference in the world.*

But when Slanger's body was lowered into the near-frozen earth of Belgium in October 1944, it was only days after a letter she'd written to the *Stars and Stripes* newspaper had melted the hearts of thousands of GIs all over Europe. So touched were they by her words of encouragement—she sent the letter only hours before she was killed when the field hospital was shelled—that hundreds wrote to the newspaper, insisting something be done to honor her. And that something was this: the finest hospital ship in the fleet was named in her honor, though Slanger never knew that.

She never knew about all the letters that poured in from GIs who said her words had instilled in them a renewed sense of hope, dignity, and purpose. She never knew the big difference she had made in their lives. But her legacy lives on as a symbol of how those who change the world, if even in small ways, are sometimes the disenfranchised, the cast-asides, the ones who toil in the shadows.

"Encourage one another and build each other up," says 1 Thessalonians 5:11. In other words, invest in one another. Realize you're necessary. Be the light for someone's darkness.

With insight into his past, Scrooge connects the dots between how we act and how our actions affect others. You get the idea that he once understood that. But somewhere between that happy Christmas Eve party at Fezziwig's and the "bah humbug" morbidity of his office on Christmas Eve, Ebenezer Scrooge lost his way.

Your Actions Affect Others

We often don't realize what a difference we make in the lives of others. What are some ways, subtle or overt, to make others feel valued?

_____

_____

_____

_____

This chapter tells the story of Frances Slanger, posthumously honored for her contribution to the World War II effort. Who are some of the people who need to be honored and acknowledged for their contributions to your life?

_____

_____

_____

The Love of Money Costs You in the End

I have seen your nobler aspirations fall
off one by one, until the master-passion,
Gain, engrosses you. Have I not?
—BELLE, EBENEZER'S LOVE INTEREST
WHEN AS A YOUNG MAN, TO HIM

On Scrooge's reunion tour with the past, a young woman, Belle, suggests Ebenezer's love for her has waned. By now Scrooge is a young man, having apparently left the employment of Fezziwig and in the process of making his way in the world of finances. "Another idol," she tells him, "has displaced me."

When she suggests his idol is now wealth, he defends his pursuit of it with a passion she probably wished had been reserved for her.

"You *are* changed," she says, breaking off their relationship.

The narrator writes the change was reflected in his face. "There was an eager, greedy, restless motion in the eye, which showed the passion that had taken root, and where the shadow of the growing tree would fall."

Decades later, the passion is gone, but the greed has grown. Scrooge clings to every pound as if it is the air he breathes. As a moneylender, his accumulation of wealth is how he controls people. To have a man owe you is to have that man in your power. He even turns his living quarters into commercial properties that he rents out.

His unspoken life philosophy mirrors many of that time and place, a reflection of what nineteenth-century Scottish philosopher Thomas Carlyle called "The Gospel of Mammonism." Success was only about how much wealth you could accumulate. Hell, lamented Carlyle in his 1843 book *Past and Present*, was "the terror of not succeeding; of not making money, fame, or some figure in the world—chiefly of making money."

In *An American Christmas Carol* (1979), Benedict Slade—played by Henry Winkler of *Happy Days* fame—is a Scrooge-like character who passes up an opportunity to take over a furniture factory because, he says, "I want to be somebody." The inference, of course, is that what defines us as people is not the richness of our relationships but some artificial criteria involving money and position. That we can't be *somebody* without hitching ourselves to the proper materialistic moorings, whose lavishness disguises the insecurity of those who desperately cling to them.

Such thinking has stolen Scrooge's soul. You don't measure materialism by how much or little you have, but on what it means to you. And to Scrooge it means everything—as it did to his partner, Jacob Marley.

Materialism shackles us to self. It diverts our attention from the things that matter most: our faith, our families, and our fundamental responsibility to help those less fortunate. It promises much but delivers little. When Scrooge mocks Fred for his sky-high Christmas Spirit—"What reason have you to be merry? You're poor enough"— Fred politely responds in kind, "What right have you to be dismal? . . . You're rich enough." The obvious irony? Poorness and richness are hardly barometers for happiness.

In the 1984 movie version of *Carol*, Scrooge's lady interest, Belle, says it well as she seeks affirmation that he loves her but realizes he does not: "There's more to life than books and ledgers. . . . How long since you danced, Ebenezer?"

"Materialism is bad for the soul," the *New York Times* reported in 2006 after research on whether it makes people happy. "Only, in the new formulation, materialism is bad for your emotional well-being [too]. In recent years, researchers have reported an ever-growing list of downsides to getting and spending—damage to relationships and self-esteem, a heightened risk of depression and anxiety, less time for what the research indicates truly makes people happy, like family, friendship and engaging work. And maybe even headaches."

Not that this should strike us as anything new. "Those who want to get rich fall into temptation and a trap and into many foolish and harmful desires that plunge people into ruin and destruction," says 1 Timothy 6:9–10. "For the love of money is a root of all kinds of evil. Some people, eager for money, have wandered from the faith and pierced themselves with many griefs."

I've always found it interesting how people make idols of money and things—the stuff that can't love them back. Perhaps you've seen the YouTube clip of the high-in-the-mountains snowmobiler with the video camera affixed to his helmet. When he crashes, we, the viewers, follow him sliding and somersaulting down the snowy mountain until he finally comes to a halt, miraculously alive.

Then, up above him, a dot in the distance appears and grows larger in the snow. It's tumbling toward him: his snowmobile, which has not come down the mountain as fast as he had. He is alive. He is with friends. He has, some would say, cheated death. But as the snowmobile comes closer to him, the man does something amazing. Instead of running *away* from it so it won't smash into him and finish off his banged-up body, he starts running *toward* the snowmobile. He's trying to corral it. Save it. Prevent it from sliding on down the mountain.

You want to yell, "Your war's over, soldier. Praise the Lord and let that hunk of metal go." But he follows it down the mountain until exhaustion overcomes him and he can go no farther.

Meanwhile, back in Scroogeville, Ebenezer admonishes the Spirit for torturing him. The Spirit is nonplussed. Scrooge still has one more stop on this sentimental journey, to a scene years later of Belle, her husband, and their wild but happy children. Amid the boisterous scene, Belle's husband mentions that he met an old friend of hers, Mr. Scrooge, that afternoon. "I passed his office window; and as it was not shut up, and he had a candle inside, I could scarcely help seeing him. His partner lies upon the point of death, I hear; and there he sat alone. Quite alone in the world, I do believe."

Perhaps the most haunting line in the chapter is a single sentence amid a thicket of reflection by Scrooge on seeing Belle and her family laughing heartily. The narrator, adding his personal thoughts on the matter, likely echoes Scrooge's when he writes, "What would I not have given to be one of them!" This lament conjures thoughts of Mark 8:36: "What good is it for someone to gain the whole world, yet forfeit their soul?"

As Scrooge softens, we readers can't help but soften toward him. He is not intrinsically bad or evil. Like us all, he's a fallen man—in his case, still suffering from abandonment and neglect as a boy. He's fearful. He's damaged. In part, because to heal his pain, he has trusted something incapable of doing so.

Nobody is saying money itself is evil. It puts food on our table, finds cures for diseases, and revitalizes communities. But when we turn to money to fill our deepest needs, it will always let us down, even if we desperately run after it until exhaustion overcomes us and we can go no farther.

It's important to note that the Bible doesn't say *money* is "a root of all kinds of evil," but rather, the *love* of money is. What does this differentiation suggest when it comes to our relationship with finances?

_____

_____

_____

_____

Exodus 32 relates the story of Moses, Aaron, and the golden calf. What are some of the idols that even today's believers encounter on their faith journey? How does God help us when we get distracted?

_____

_____

_____

LESSON 15

"Almost" Doesn't Cut It

I almost went after her.
—Scrooge, in the 1984 movie version, to the Ghost of
Christmas Past after Belle breaks up with Ebenezer

In big things and small, Scrooge plays life safe. He worries about keeping every shilling he has. He worries about a chunk of coal being too much for the office fire. And he acts as if a smile might physically hurt.

The 1984 movie version of *A Christmas Carol* suggests Scrooge's take-no-risks approach to life may have begun the day Belle confronted him about his feelings—or lack thereof—toward her. In the book, the scene ends with her saying, "May you be happy in the life you have chosen!" And they part.

In the movie, Scrooge says to the Ghost of Christmas Past, "I almost went after her," after which the Spirit replies, "Almost carries no weight, especially in matters of the heart."

Wise Spirit, this. Reminds me of a similar quote: "Not to decide is to decide."

If anyone should live life adventurously, shouldn't it be those of us who claim to follow Jesus? We have a relationship with the God of the universe, who's promised to be with us every step of the way. Instead, too many of us cloister ourselves with other believers, dare not venture into anything that might take us out of our comfort zones, and become far too content with monetary security, television, and risk-free choices.

This from people whom Oswald Chambers says should be living life with "reckless joy."

"Life can be either a nightmare or an adventure," a pastor, author, and friend of mine is fond of saying.

To live life as a nightmare is to doubt God's promises, which leaves little alternative than to accept the world's promises, however unreliable they have proven, which Scrooge learns the hard way with Belle.

To live it as an adventure is to live with the confidence that God is trustworthy—and less concerned with our choices than whether we're making those choices with our hearts in the right places and with the faith to believe he will guide and protect us.

It means fighting against the mundaneness of a material life. It means choosing not to live with follow-the-leader redundancy but with adventurous faith. It means eschewing a play-it-safe mentality in favor of a let's-see-if-this-works mentality.

Too many Christians are utterly fearful of failure. Fortunately, there are exceptions. Decades ago, long before I attended it, our church was forced to leave a space it rented at the local fairgrounds because the structure had been condemned. After much prayer, the elders decided to forge ahead with a risky plan to buy land and to build. Some of them went so far as to mortgage their homes to secure the loan; that, dear reader, is living beyond "almost."

And then came the bad news: the city's building code required far more dirt for this marshy land than our elders had anticipated, so expenses were going to be much higher. Did the church leaders quit? No. They prayed.

The phone rang. Our local hospital, a Catholic-run institute, was building a parking garage and having to dig a deep hole to do so. Hospital officials had heard our church could use dirt. The hospital could save big money if it didn't have to haul the dirt far out of town. *Could you use some free dirt?*

I have long joked that we are a Protestant church built on a Catholic foundation. Why, nearly forty years later, do we have one of our community's more vibrant places of worship? In part because our church leaders, long ago, didn't "almost" decide to build a new church building.

Jesus was a radical. He mixed it up with the riffraff. Stepped out of boats onto water. Turned water into wine. If we are to emulate

Him, why do we trust God so little that we, too, play it safe, our words saying we trust Him but our actions not?

Especially in things of the heart.

Sometimes it's difficult to think of our walk with God as an adventure. What are some examples from Jesus' ministry that suggest that faith can be adventurous and exciting?

_____

_____

_____

_____

Fear of failure is a common response to any undertaking that involves risk or sacrifice. How is failure a natural part of simply being human, and how does God help us when we fail or fall short of expectations?

_____

_____

_____

Life Is Best Lived When You're Awake

I never noticed that.

—Scrooge, in the 1984 movie version, after the Ghost of Christmas Past points out that Belle "resembled your sister"

Scrooge's life went astray sometime when he was a young man. We can, with reasonable certainty, say he didn't wake up one morning and think, *Hm. I'm content where I am. I'm enjoying my apprenticeship with Old Fezziwig. I'm in love with a beautiful young woman. I have friends. But I think I'll begin morphing into a money-centric fool who loses his way, gives up his girl, cuts off his friendships, and winds up as a bitter old miser living in a drafty old house, my life utterly devoid of the slightest semblance of joy—even if it would make a great book by, say, Charles Dickens, assuming I were visited by four eccentric Ghosts.*

No, it happened insidiously, as if one of the tires on our car gets out of alignment and starts to wear heavily on the outside edge. But we don't check on it. And the problem gets worse. It affects the other tires. Soon our steering wheel shakes like an out-of-kilter washing machine agitator, and our car is unsafe to drive. Either that or we crash.

In the 1984 movie version, the Ghost of Christmas Present calls out Scrooge for letting life pass him by. "You've gone through life not noticing a lot," the Spirit says. In the same movie version, at the end, Scrooge tells his nephew Fred, "I see the shadow of your mother in your face. I forgot how much I loved her. Perhaps I chose to forget."

We need to live intentionally, with our antennae up. We need to notice our life as we're living it. Why? For three reasons.

The first is to appreciate all that God has blessed us with. Given the chance to live their lives again, fifty octogenarians were asked by sociology professor and author Tony Campolo what they would do differently. They said they would risk more, would do more things that would live on after they were dead, and would reflect more on the journey while they were on it.

To not pay attention is to miss the wonder of being alive. To miss the people around us, the needs around us, and the beauty around us. And we miss the umbrella above it all: the God who loves us unconditionally.

In these days of multitasking, social media, and dawn-to-dusk rushing around, I wonder if we're going too fast to pay attention. Or if we've fooled ourselves into believing that we're accomplishing so much, when what we're really doing is making treasure of the trivial—immersing ourselves in making money, for example, at the expense of building relationships. Or if subconsciously we *purposely* go too fast—to avoid having to face a compulsive "us" that we might not want to face.

Dickens grew up as a keen observer of the world and his place in it. Sickly and frail, he was much more spectator than athlete. "He loved to watch people at church, in the market, at school," writes Norrie Epstein, author of *The Friendly Dickens*. Not surprisingly, he became a writer, an observer of—and commentator on—the human condition.

In Thornton Wilder's *Our Town*, Emily, who died while giving birth to her second child, is given a chance to witness the day she turned twelve. In doing so, she realizes all the nuances of life she would never again see.

"It goes so fast," she says. "We don't have time to look at one another. Goodbye world. . . . Goodbye to clocks ticking . . . and Mama's sunflowers. And food and coffee. And new-ironed dresses and hot baths . . . and sleeping and waking up. Oh, earth, you're too wonderful for anybody to realize you . . . Do any human beings ever realize life while they live it—every, every minute?"

"No," replies the stage manager, then pauses. "The saints and poets, maybe—they do some."

Second, we need to notice what's going on around us so we can be there for others. Thomas Hood, in an article appearing a year after *A Christmas Carol* was released, wondered if, like Scrooge, "our own heads have not become more inaccessible, our hearts more impregnable, our ears and eyes more dull and blind, to sounds and sights of human misery."

We can't help others if we don't notice their needs. In the 1938 *Christmas Carol* movie, starring Reginald Owen as Scrooge, the Ghost of Jacob Marley tells Ebenezer, "Each day a man has a thousand chances to make right." But not if that man doesn't notice those opportunities.

Finally, we need to notice what's going on around us to keep us headed in the right direction in our lives. I was sailing in the San Juan Islands off Washington State, deep in conversation with my sailing buddy. Suddenly I realized we were far off course. Why? Tides had shifted, and I had been too preoccupied to notice.

So, too, did the tides shift in Scrooge's life. Perhaps he could have compensated had he kept his eyes on the headland where he was originally aimed and noticed the shifting tides in his life. But once we lose sight of land, once we can't see—or won't notice—where we're headed, the shoals grow hungry for the catch.

Said Albert Einstein, "He to whom the emotion is a stranger, who can no longer pause to wonder and stand wrapped in awe, is as good as dead; his eyes are closed."

In today's hectic world, it's easy to forget to stop and simply be grateful. List some of the things you are thankful God has given you and offer up a brief prayer of gratitude for each one.

_____

_____

_____

_____

If life were a rushing river, would you rather be standing on the banks or on a raft moving with the current? What are the pros and cons of each scenario?

_____

_____

_____

Fear Has a Downside*

You fear the world too much.

—Belle, to a young Ebenezer, as they part ways

With a deft balance of forthrightness and reserve—and fueled by more than a little courage—Belle lays it on the line with a young Scrooge in a telling Christmas Past scene. "You've given up on your of love of me," she effectively says, "for the pursuit of money."

With a deft balance between pride and shame—and fueled by more than a little insecurity—young Ebenezer fires back.

"There is nothing on which it is so hard as poverty," he says, "and there is nothing it professes to condemn with such severity as the pursuit of wealth!"

---

*Fear not. Fear also has an upside. See lesson 27.

It is here that Belle offers a subtle but oh-so-insightful line: "You fear the world too much."

The narrator tells us she says it "gently," but her probing insight hits its intended target. Scrooge doesn't deny it, rationalizing that it's only a sign of him having—*ahem*—"Grown so much wiser." He then quickly changes the subject to weakly deny that his feelings for her have changed.

Fear can stifle us. Fear can blind us to the things that matter most. Fear can force us to rely on material things rather than on heart things for our security.

Lest we seem too harsh on the young Scrooge, let's acknowledge the elephant in the room: the guy has separation-anxiety issues. He had been sent away to a boarding school, much like Dickens himself had been sent off to work as a boy. When everyone else went home for Christmas break, Scrooge stayed at the boarding school, alone.

That's not all. Scrooge's father, even if he's had a change of heart, had been cruel. And, though not spelled out by Dickens, his mother has likely died.

The result? He's an insecure young man. Other than his sister, Fan, whom he seldom sees; and a friend at Fezziwig's, Dick Wilkins; Scrooge has little in the way of meaningful human connections. Yet blessed with the opportunity to break the chains of family dysfunction and start anew with exactly that—with a woman who seems altogether "together"—he chooses "Gain" instead.

That's the fear speaking. The insecurity. The lack of faith in the unseen.

Why do we run away from the stuff we need and into the arms of the stuff that can never satisfy our deepest needs?

Fear.

As believers, we might say we trust God to meet our needs, but our actions often suggest otherwise. We might think we're all about relationships, but our priorities suggest otherwise. We might pretend that we don't need it all, but our choices suggest otherwise. Never mind that Scripture says we can't serve God and money, that our priorities are to be relationships, that, in essence, we can't take it with us. Fear tells us to follow the leader, and so we—as did Scrooge—allow ourselves to be helplessly carried by the cultural currents.

"Acting on your faith is the ultimate expression of devotion, admiration, and adoration," writes Andy Stanley in *Visioneering*. "Acting on your faith demonstrates that you believe God is who he says he is, and he will do what he has promised to do."

Belle calls Scrooge's bluff. He musters a pseudo-noble defense, but it's what he *doesn't* say that speaks so loudly. He's made his choice.

Panning to a broader time perspective, we can see that Scrooge's choice hardens his heart for years to come, memories of the past steeling his resolve to believe love is a waste of time. In the first stave, after Scrooge questions his nephew about why he married, Fred says it was because he fell in love.

"Because you *fell in love*," scoffs Scrooge, with unabashed derision, his insecurity tucked safely behind his curmudgeonly pride.

Ah, but what happens when the Ghost strips Scrooge bare of such pride, when it shows Belle and her happy family to Ebenezer? He laments what might have been—had he not given in to fear.

Second Timothy 1:7 says that "God has not given us a spirit of fear, but of power and of love and of a sound mind" (NKJV). Compare a time when you handled something out of fear versus a time when you responded with love. What did you learn from both situations?

_____

_____

_____

_____

Our life is comprised of a long string of choices, some good, some bad. If you could travel back in time, how would you change some of your not-so-great decisions?

_____

_____

_____

LESSON 18

Showing Trumps Telling

The Spirit touched him on the arm, and
pointed to his younger self . . .
—THE GHOST OF CHRISTMAS PAST, ENCOURAGING
SCROOGE TO LOOK AT THE OLD "HIM"

As Scrooge listens to his tour guide, notice how the Spirit doesn't lecture Ebenezer on his botched life; instead, it shows Scrooge's life to him and lets him learn the lessons on his own. Telling is good, but showing is better.

Dickens himself was a good example. Certainly his books had political and social bents meant to comfort the afflicted and afflict the comfortable, but the author lived out his values beyond his books. "Charles Dickens," writes Jane Smiley in *Charles Dickens* (2002), "was not only a famous author, he was also a self-conscious and responsible citizen who never forgot that fame gave him an unusual opportunity to comment upon and influence political events. Already, by 1839, at the age of twenty-seven, Dickens was being honored by his friends for active benevolence."

Showing speaks louder than telling. It's a lesson I teach writing students with vigor. Mark Twain said it best: "Don't say the old lady screamed. Bring her on and let her scream." Sermons with five alliterated points reach us at an intellectual level. A testimony from a prodigal son grabs our heart and won't let go.

Says James 1:22, "Do not merely listen to the word, and so deceive yourselves. Do what it says." In other words, don't tell the world you're a believer; *show* them. Sure, you can slap a fish symbol on the back of your car and stake a "He Is Risen" sign in your yard come Easter, but it'll mean more to your neighbors if you loan them tools, help them build their rock wall, and bring them a meal when they are convalescing after surgery.

You can say you're a woman of God, but it means nothing if you don't walk the talk. Likewise, you can tell your girlfriend you love her deeply, but it will mean more if you arrive unexpectedly at her door after a five-hour drive from college, bearing a large pepperoni pizza, a dozen red roses, and a homemade card with "I love you" spelled out from the cereal letters in a box of Alpha-Bits.

Scrooge is starting to get it. His trip back in time evokes the same sort of emotions we feel when we page through an old photo album. Some of it makes us laugh. Some of it brings lumps to our throats. Some of it triggers regret. But all of it leaves us different than it found us.

So showing is a double-edged sword: seeing the past can make us hurt and can help us heal. But some people don't understand short-term pain for the long-term gain. They find it easier—not better in the long run, just easier—to pretend that those good times never happened. In Scrooge's case, it's easier for him to rationalize that darkness is cheap—he could afford more gas lamps outside his house but eschewed them because of cost—than to face the conviction that he has turned his back on the light.

Showing is powerful. It cuts through all the rhetoric and locks on to our heart like a heat-seeking missile.

Ouch.

It gives Scrooge the perspective he's been afraid to revisit all these years: *what might have been* contrasted against *what actually was.*

Ouch.

It reconnects him with feelings he hasn't experienced since then. For example, he experiences goodness—at the Spirit's unveiling of the Fezziwig party, you'd have thought Scrooge was actually *there*, so real was the experience of returning for him. For the first time in forever, Scrooge remembers the pleasure of enjoying himself, something that men who eat gruel alone on Christmas Eve aren't accustomed to doing.

Ouch.

Yes, being shown the past hurts Scrooge terribly. "Leave me," he tells the Ghost of Christmas Past. "Take me back. Haunt me no more." Ah, but remember Dickens wrote *A Christmas Carol* in part to have a disquieting effect on us. To make us think. To make us reconsider. "May it haunt [your house] pleasantly," he tells us in the preface.

In a sense, that's what the Spirits are doing to Scrooge. They are savvy Spirits. And while there's no suggestion they are God-breathed or heaven-sent, they know what some of us know well: it's not until we're shown the errors of our old ways that we can find a new way.

What if you could come face-to-face with the old "you"? What kind of advice would you give your younger self?

_____

_____

_____

_____

Why is *showing* someone the truth often so much more effective than *telling* someone the truth?

_____

_____

_____

LESSON 19

Learning Begins with Listening

"Spirit," said Scrooge submissively,
"conduct me where you will."
—SCROOGE, UPON MEETING THE GHOST
OF CHRISTMAS PRESENT

Scrooge's reception to each of the three Ghosts suggests a gradual dropping of his guard, softening of his heart, and opening of his mind.

He initially doubts Marley's Ghost is even real. "Humbug, I tell you—humbug!" And even when he comes to believe it *is* real, Scrooge considers it a bother. "Dreadful apparition, why do you trouble me?"

He is still a touch resistant with the Ghost of Christmas Past. "Who, and what are you?" But that fades. The Spirit, exuding a certain childlike quality, assures him it has come for Scrooge's "welfare" and "reclamation," and it clasps Ebenezer gently by the arm in preparation for their walk down memory lane.

When the Ghost of Christmas Present arrives—a "jolly giant" dressed in a Christmasy green robe accented with holly—Scrooge appears resigned to wherever it might lead. Ebenezer looks upon it "reverently" and later says, "Spirit, conduct me where you will."

He even begins asking the Spirit questions and introduces a touch of humor in the conversation. "Have you had many brothers, Spirit?"

"More than eighteen hundred."

"A tremendous family to provide for!" says Scrooge. Yes, a touch of levity from Scrooge. What's getting into him? Next thing we know he's going to be a guest on the 1840s version of *The Tonight Show with Jimmy Fallon*.

Whatever these Spirits are up to, Scrooge is beginning to realize, they seem to have his best interest in mind. "I went forth last night on compulsion, and I learnt a lesson which is working now," he says, referring to his trip with the Ghost of Christmas Past.

That's quite a change from his humbug attitude toward Marley's Ghost. And what's behind that change? His realization that when you stop to listen, you learn. And when you're being taught by those who care about your welfare, it's to your advantage to keep paying attention.

"The way of fools seems right to them," says Proverbs 12:15, "but the wise listen to advice." And James 1:19: "Everyone should be quick to listen, slow to speak and slow to become angry."

I used to think I was a good listener. I taught journalism students the art of interviewing. Amid the myriad things going on in a conversation, I would tell them, hearing what the person is saying is paramount. Then, as my wife, Sally, and I were going through training to help launch a marriage coaching team at our church, I realized something: with her, I start to listen, but only as a means of gathering enough information so I can formulate an opinion and convince her I'm right.

I had been writing newspaper columns for nearly forty years. You do your research, formulate your thesis, and politely suggest the reader look at things your way. I realized subconsciously that's what I was doing in conversations with Sally.

I wasn't listening to her. I was positioning myself to win an argument. Listening, I've come to realize, isn't about *me*. It's about whoever is talking. It's about learning. It's not judging. It's not using the information as ammunition for an argument. It's trying to understand where someone else is coming from and using that information to be a better spouse, friend, mentor—whatever.

"To answer before listening—that is folly and shame," says Proverbs 18:13.

I'm not sure I've come as far as Scrooge does. Really, you have to give the guy credit. He starts out more resistant to these Ghosts than werewolves to fire and, by Ghost number three, has acquiesced to the Spirits' leading.

"To-night," he tells the Ghost of Christmas Present, "if you have aught to teach me, let me profit by it."

It's one thing to hear what someone is saying, but to listen to them takes a lot more effort. What are some ways you can start listening more effectively to the people around you?

_____

_____

_____

_____

The Ghosts in *A Christmas Carol* are beginning to chip away at Scrooge's resistance. Why do we resist change so vigorously, and what are some ways to be more open to God's adjustments in our lives?

_____

_____

_____

LESSON 20

Blessed Are the Poor

God bless us, every one!
—Tiny Tim, as witnessed by Scrooge and
the Ghost of Christmas Present

If the Ghost of Christmas Present had been afforded frequent-flier miles, he would have cashed in big-time on his stint with Scrooge. The two visit a marketplace, a miners' cottage, a lighthouse, a ship, and the home of Fred.

The theme, if jollier, is less personal than the Ghost of Christmas Past offers. The Ghost of Christmas Present wants to give Scrooge perspective on the poor, showing how they rise above their meager conditions to celebrate the Christmas season. Just as the movie *Titanic* exhorts the virtues of the lower class by showing the folks in steerage having all the fun while the wealthy up top complain and cackle about this and that, so does *A Christmas Carol* suggest a certain grit, dignity, and optimism among the poor.

At the time *A Christmas Carol* was written, 1843, the disenfranchised were struggling to feed their families amid England's draconian rules that forced many impoverished people into prisons and—as Scrooge himself mentioned—workhouses. Conditions for the lower class were horrid. People without fireplaces would set fires anyway in an attempt to keep warm. At the time, a third of all deaths in London were estimated to be of children. In the 1840s, London was such a place of haves and have-nots that novelist and politician Benjamin Disraeli referred to his country as made up of "two nations, the rich and the poor."

Dickens once visited a "ragged school," part of a movement to provide basic instruction for poor children. "I have very seldom seen in all the strange and dreadful things I have seen in London and elsewhere, anything so shocking as the dire neglect of soul and body exhibited in these children," he wrote.

But Dickens looks for the hope in the hopeless, looks for the good in people, looks not so much at *what is* but *what might be*, even if it might take a bit of fairy dust from the Ghost of Christmas Present's torch—an allusion to the Holy Spirit?—to make it happen.

Yes, Dickens sentimentalized the plight of the poor, particularly in the use of Tiny Tim. But he did so with a purpose: that his words might raise awareness about the plight of the poor and help change

England's inhumane system. "There is a great man who makes every man feel small," writes G. K. Chesterton in *Charles Dickens: The Last of the Great Men*. "But the real great man is the man who makes every man feel great."

Virtue "dwells rather oftener in alleys and byways than she does in courts and palaces," Dickens once said. He knew. Not only did his early newspaper career afford him looks at London's seamier side, but he had also lived in that world himself. Dickens grew up in the same Camden Town where he places the Cratchits. He could relate to the loss of Tiny Tim; he had lost two siblings himself. And early on, he was brought up by a father who resembled Scrooge's father; the man "was an unmitigated disaster," writes Norrie Epstein in *The Friendly Dickens*. The family moved more than twenty times in eighteen years. Charles had seen them physically evicted for nonpayment of rent.

Thus, amid the cold-knuckle plight of those in poverty, Dickens paints the Christmas Spirit rising above the strife in places that don't conjure thoughts of cheer. Here we are in the marketplace, where grocers and customers alike are in "the best humor possible"; here we are at a miners' cottage, "a cheerful company assembled around a glowing fire"; and here we are at a lighthouse where the two light-keepers wish each other Merry Christmas with a toast of grog.

When Scrooge asks the Ghost of Christmas Present how it decides on whom to sprinkle from its torch of goodwill, the Spirit says, "To any kindly given. To a poor one most."

"Why to a poor one most?" asks Scrooge.

"Because it needs it most."

Dickens's passion for the poor mirrors that of Scripture, which includes more than three hundred verses on the poor and social justice, and God's concern for both. "Blessed are you who hunger now, for you will be satisfied," said Jesus. "Blessed are you who weep now, for you will laugh" (Luke 6:21).

Clearly, the poor have a special place in the heart of God. "Has not God chosen those who are poor in the eyes of the world to be rich in faith and to inherit the kingdom he promised those who love him?" (James 2:5).

The rich's shabby treatment of the poor is hardly news to God. "Is it not the rich who are exploiting you? Are they not the ones who are dragging you into court? Are they not the ones who are blaspheming the noble name of him to whom you belong?" (James 2:6–7).

Most of us live our lives somewhere in the middle, neither rich nor poor. But *A Christmas Carol* seems less concerned with the bottom line of our personal ledgers than the bottom line of our hearts. The book subtly asks: Who are you? Giver or taker? Proud or humble? The Scrooge before enlightenment or the Scrooge we now see in transition to something greater?

Read Zechariah 7:8–10. Why is looking after the "foreigner or the poor" such an integral part of following Christ? What does it suggest about the human tendency toward selfishness and pride?

_____

_____

_____

_____

What are some effective ways to help those in need within your community this holiday season?

_____

_____

_____

LESSON 21

Attitude Is Everything

There was nothing very cheerful in the climate or the
town, and yet was there an air of cheerfulness abroad.
—The narrator, from a scene the Ghost of
Christmas Present shows Scrooge

In this scene from Christmas Present, the narrator paints the world as if the brush were in the hand of Norman Rockwell himself: everything a bit rosier than it actually was, the smiles brighter, the Christmas greetings lustier. And nowhere is the Spirit more alive than at Bob Cratchit's home.

Never mind that Cratchit makes the equivalent of thirty-three dollars a week in today's US dollars. That Mrs. Cratchit wears a "twice-turned gown." And that the family lives in a four-room house with six children. When a daughter, Martha, arrives late, Mrs. Cratchit kisses her "a dozen times." When the conversation rolls around to their Christmas goose, the children get positively giddy. When Bob proposes a toast at dinner's end, all raise their glasses without hesitation.

"A Merry Christmas to us all, my dears," toasts Bob to his family. "God bless us."

"God bless us every one!" says Tiny Tim, despite having a life-threatening disease and having to use a crutch because of a bad leg.

This from a family that doesn't appear to have much reason to be cheerful. "They were not a handsome family," writes the narrator. "They were not well dressed; their shoes were far from being water-proof; their clothes were scanty. . . . But they were happy, grateful, pleased with one another, and contented with the time."

Indeed, the Cratchits are a far cry from today's Facebook posters who rant about someone getting their parking spot or cutting in the grocery store line. But Dickens's message is the stuff of Philippians 4:11–12, Paul's thesis that contentment isn't about circumstances but about our attitude overriding circumstances.

"I am not saying this because I am in need," Paul writes, "for I have learned to be content whatever the circumstances. I know what it is to be in need, and I know what it is to have plenty. I have learned the secret of being content in any and every situation, whether well fed or hungry, whether living in plenty or in want."

In nearly forty years in journalism, I've been granted access to thousands of lives and I can tell you this: there is little connection between people's circumstances and their contentedness—or to be fair, their *apparent* contentedness, since I'm not privy to the depths of human hearts. But one of the most content, giving, courageous people I've written about lost her husband, daughter, and dog in an auto accident that she survived. And one of the most discontented people I've written about was a millionaire who lived on a sun-splashed lake and constantly fought with a neighbor over the height of the shrubs dividing their two houses—and later took his own life.

"Words can never adequately convey the incredible impact of our attitude toward life," begins pastor Chuck Swindoll's well-known analysis of attitude. "The longer I live the more convinced I become that life is 10 percent what happens to us and 90 percent how we respond to it. I believe the single most significant decision I can make on a day-to-day basis is my choice of attitude. It is more important than my past, my education, my bankroll, my successes or failures, fame or pain, what other people think of me or say about me, my circumstances, or my position. Attitude keeps me going or cripples my progress. It alone fuels my fire or assaults my hope. When my attitudes are right, there's no barrier too high, no valley too deep, no dream too extreme, no challenge too great for me."

Just ask the Cratchits.

As the saying goes, money can't buy happiness. List some of the things in your life that money can't buy. Offer up a brief prayer of thanks for each one.

_____

_____

_____

_____

A good attitude can go a long way, even in the most challenging of circumstances. Think of a recent situation in which you could have had a better attitude, or one in which God helped you maintain a positive perspective. What did you learn?

_____

_____

_____

LESSON 22

Talking the Talk Is Not Enough

If these shadows remain unaltered by
the Future, the child will die.
—The Ghost of Christmas Present to Scrooge, as
they witness Tiny Tim and the Cratchit family

It is one of the signature scenes in *A Christmas Carol*—the sobering news of Tiny Tim's future should nothing be done to change his present course, and the Spirit implying that Scrooge can alter that course.

Earlier, Scrooge has seen Bob Cratchit enter the family home with Tim on his shoulder. Later, a single moment triggers a foreboding thought in Scrooge. Tim sits close to his father, who holds his "withered little hand in his, as if he loved the child, and wished to keep him by his side, and dreaded that he might be taken from him."

Scrooge is anxious—almost desperate—to know: Will Tiny Tim live?

"If these shadows remain unaltered by the Future, the child will die," says the Spirit.

When Scrooge responds with anguish—"Say he will be spared"—the Ghost of Christmas Present twists the knife of guilt deep into Scrooge's gut, playing off a comment Ebenezer had made to dissuade the alms-for-the-poor solicitors at his office Christmas Eve. If the boy dies, says the Spirit sarcastically, it will "decrease the surplus population."

The Ghost of Christmas Present is putting the onus on Scrooge: *If this kid is going to live, it will be because you intervene and see to it that he gets the care he needs. And if this kid dies, his blood is on your hands.* In other words, wishing the boy good thoughts, worrying about his future, and being empathetic to his needs is not enough. *You need to do something, pal.*

When contrasting this scene to the biblical call to be "doers of the word" (James 1:22 KJV), there's one important difference and one important similarity between the two.

The difference is that the Spirit is imploring action from a man who's never lifted a finger to help anyone else in his life. On the other hand, followers of Jesus, ostensibly, seek to do that on a regular basis. But James, in his "doer of the word" reference, would not be imploring the masses to such a standard if they were already doing it, which, obviously, they were not. And we are not.

The similarity is that the important thing here is not feelings, thoughts, how much faith you have, or, in Scrooge's case at this point, how little faith you have. What's important is *action*. Love, as they say, is a verb.

"What good is it, my brothers and sisters, if someone claims to have faith but has no deeds? Can such faith save them? Suppose a brother or a sister is without clothes and daily food. If one of you says to them, 'Go in peace; keep warm and well fed,' but does nothing about their physical needs, what good is it? In the same way, faith by itself, if it is not accompanied by action, is dead" (James 2:14–17).

Dickens was far more interested in deeds than dogma. He battled vigilantly for the rights of the poor, established funds to aid orphans, and taught his own children the value of Jesus' example. Even in his last will and testament of June 2, 1870, he exhorted his children to "guide themselves by the teaching of the New Testament in its broad Spirit, and to put no faith in any man's narrow construction of its letters here or there."

When criticized for his harshness toward Christians who, in his estimation, weren't being "doers of the word," Dickens replied that his focus was on hypocrisy, not on people: "I have so strong an objection to mere professions of religion, and to the audacious interposition of vain and ignorant men between the sublime simplicity of the New Testament and the general human mind to which our Savior addressed it, that I urge that objection as strongly and as positively as I can."

If we are made in the image of God and God clearly has a heart for the poor, then shouldn't we be doing more to take care of the poor? I know believers who have dedicated their lives to serving the poor, but I also know believers who look at the poor with disdain and fear, far more worried that a dollar handed out on a street corner might be spent on booze than whether its would-be recipient has, say, eaten in the last week.

"Sell your possessions and give to the poor," Jesus said in Luke 12:33–34. In other words, *take action*. "Provide purses for yourselves that will not wear out, a treasure in heaven that will never fail, where no thief comes near and no moth destroys. For where your treasure is, there your heart will be also."

Michael Fechner took that verse seriously. Fechner, who died of cancer in 2014, was a self-described Christian "pretender," a Mercedes-driving Dallas millionaire. After being inspired by the deep—and far more genuine than his own—faith of a single mom in an iron-bar neighborhood in South Dallas, he made a U-turn in life. He sold essentially all he had, started a ministry called BridgeBuilders, and dedicated his life to serving the poor, all for the glory of a God he once saw as his personal genie but realized was so much more.

Why the change? He was tired of playing the good-Christian game. He started seeing the poor not as a problem but as God-created people. Indeed, it was as if the Holy Spirit said to him, "I see an empty chair at the table" and, instead of looking around for someone else to take responsibility for others, the man stepped up himself.

If not us, who?

The author repeats the familiar phrase "Love is a verb." What exactly does this mean for you as you contemplate your own life?

_____

_____

_____

_____

Sometimes putting your faith into action is easier said than done. What are some small changes you can make to become a person who acts on faith rather than standing on the sidelines?

_____

_____

_____

The Past Can Be Empowering

*He told me, coming home, that he hoped the people
saw him in the church, because he was a cripple, and it
might be pleasant to them to remember upon Christmas
Day, who made lame beggars walk and blind men see.*
—Bob Cratchit, on a comment from Tiny
Tim on their way home from church

Charles Dickens's faith is reflected in his writing, in how he conducted his life, and in his legacy, part of which manifested itself in the book on Jesus he wrote for his children a few years after *A Christmas Carol* was published.

In it, Dickens expounds on the gospel of Luke. "He wanted his children to learn about the life and teachings of Jesus Christ in as plain and simple a way as possible," writes a great-great-grandson, Gerald Charles Dickens, "and he decided the best way to achieve that was to write it himself and give it to his family as a gift."

Dickens was saying to his children, *Remember. We're a part of a story that begins in the past. Remember the words Jesus gave to us. Remember the example He left for us. Remember the expectations He has for us.*

Lest anyone think it was a veiled attempt to make money, Dickens mandated that the book not be published in his lifetime. Upon his death, in 1870, the book was passed to his sister-in-law, who passed it on to Dickens's last-surviving son, Henry Fielding Dickens, whose will gave his heirs the freedom to decide whether the book should be published. In 1934, they decided it was time, and Simon & Schuster published the first American edition of *The Life of Our Lord.*

"It outlines his faith, which was simple and deeply held," writes Gerald Dickens.

In particular, the book emphasizes Jesus' mercy, miracles, and forgiveness. "My Dear Children," it begins, "I am very anxious that you should know something about the History of Jesus Christ. For everybody ought to know about him."

After telling the story of the prodigal son, Dickens writes, "By this, Our Savior meant to teach that those who have done wrong and forgotten God, are always welcome to Him and will always receive his mercy, if they will only return to Him in sorrow for the sin of which they have been guilty."

The book championed Dickens's concern for the poor. "Never

be proud or unkind, my dears, to any poor man, woman or child. If they are bad, think that they would have been better if they had had kind friends, and good homes, and had been better taught. . . . When people speak ill of the poor and miserable, think how Jesus Christ went among them, and taught them, and thought them worthy of His care."

The book trumpeted Jesus' miracles. "When he came out of the wilderness, He began to cure sick people by only laying His hand upon them," wrote Dickens, "for God had given Him power to heal the sick, and to give sight to the blind."

Which brings us to Tiny Tim, who tells his father on the way home from church that "he hoped the people saw him in the church, because he was a cripple, and it might be pleasant to them to remember upon Christmas Day, who made lame beggars walk and blind men see."

Pretty inspiring stuff for a character who most believe was about six years old at the time. In this insightful statement, he uses the same word that underscores why Dickens took time to write a book on Jesus for his children and, you could argue, helps Scrooge rethink his life:

Remember.

Read the parable of the prodigal son (Luke 15:11–31). Why do you think this story is so beloved among believers? What does it teach us about selfishness? About sin and pride? About forgiveness?

_____

_____

_____

_____

Miracles still happen. They may not be "big" miracles like walking on water or healing the blind, but they still make a big difference. Think of the small miracles that have happened in your life in the past two weeks. What ripple effect did they have, and how did they change you?

_____

_____

_____

Don't Return Evil for Evil

*A Merry Christmas and a Happy New
Year to the old man, wherever he is!*
—Fred, toasting his uncle only hours after Scrooge
rebuked him for being giddy about Christmas

The Ghost of Christmas Present's stopovers at the homes of Bob
Cratchit and Fred are notable for lots of reasons, not the least of
which is parallel responses from the two men toward Scrooge despite
Ebenezer having treated them so shabbily. Not only does neither
demand an eye for an eye, but both defend him in front of spouses
who loathe the old miser more than stale figgy pudding.

Think about it. Cratchit was made to feel guilty for wanting
Christmas Day off. The way Scrooge went nutty you'd think his clerk

had asked for a hundred-pound raise and a company-paid vacation in the south of France. And Fred's Christmas joviality was met by Scrooge with spite, sarcasm, and snideness—the same trio he used to rain on his nephew's subsequent pro-love-and-marriage parade.

Sure, it's Christmas Eve, but you could understand if instead of taking a snow slide with the neighborhood boys and engaging his kids in a game of blindman's buff, Cratchit had arrived home with all the Christmas Eve levity of George Bailey in *It's a Wonderful Life*. Maybe kicked over a few things in the living room and yelled at the kids.

You could understand why Fred might have shown up at Scrooge's house that evening and decorated the knocker on his uncle's front door with what looked like a festive bouquet of mistletoe but was actually poison oak.

But instead we hear this from Cratchit: "a Christmas Eve toast to Mr. Scrooge, the Founder of the Feast!" His wife, incredulous, rears up like a horse that's just been bitten by a rattlesnake. "I wish I had him here. I'd give him a piece of my mind to feast upon, and I hope he'd have a good appetite for it."

Same way at Fred's place: "I couldn't be angry with him if I tried," Fred says. His wife and others harrumph in unison. "I have no patience with him," huffs his wife.

We can credit Bob and Fred for responses straight from the Scriptures: "Do not repay evil with evil or insult with insult. On the contrary, repay evil with blessing, because to this you were called so that you may inherit a blessing" (1 Peter 3:9).

Don't Return Evil for Evil

Dickens said as much in the book he wrote for his children. He wrote of God's forgiveness, then told his children, "We must always forgive those who have done us any harm, when they come to us and say they are truly sorry for it. Even if they do not come and say so, we must still forgive them, and never hate them or be unkind to them, if we would hope that God will forgive us."

We've all heard "Two wrongs don't make a right." Forgiveness is a pillar of the Christian walk. What are the ramifications of unforgiveness, both in us and the person we choose not to forgive?

_____

_____

_____

_____

Read Matthew 5:38–39. Think of a time when you turned the other cheek or a situation where you chose not to. What did you learn from either situation?

_____

_____

_____

LESSON 25

Bitterness Will Poison You

Who suffers by his ill whims! Himself, always.
—FRED, REGARDING HIS UNCLE DURING THE
GHOST OF CHRISTMAS PRESENT VISIT

Bitterness has its victims, and Fred reminds us, the victim is the one spewing the bitterness, not the one at whom the venom is aimed. Scrooge's "offences carry their own punishment," he says.

That punishment is what?

"The consequences of his taking a dislike to us, and not making merry with us, is, I think, that he loses some pleasant moments, which could do him no harm. I am sure he loses pleasanter companions than he can find in his own thoughts."

He's right. Walling ourselves off from people costs us

relationships that might enrich us. We also pay a price when we're the victims of bitterness and choose to bite back instead of accepting that some people are discontent and, at times, we get in their line of fire.

Jesus hung out with the poor, the outcast, the lonely, prostitutes, tax collectors, Samaritans, women caught in adultery, lepers, cheats, thieves, drunkards, idolaters, and murderers. Plenty of people who, if we're grading on a curve, might make Scrooge seem deserving of London's First Citizen award. Why? Because Jesus saw them as hurting people whose only hope of changing is by loving them— right where they *are*—into the kingdom. And by being a model of God's love.

Isn't that how Fred looks at Scrooge? "He may rail at Christmas till he dies, but he can't help thinking better of it—I defy him—if he finds me going there, in good temper, year after year, and saying Uncle Scrooge, how are you?" Ever the optimist, Fred believes in leading by example, despite the odds.

Bitterness can also make the deliverer bitter. Even though it feels good to vent back at a person, that feeling quickly dissipates. The result? We've dug the divide between us and the offender deeper. What's more, wallowing in self-pity only hurts you. Bitterness, it's been said, is like swallowing poison and hoping that the other person will die.

Been there, done that. For years, a particular reader had taken me to task for errors he perceived in my columns. Most of the time he was right. What galled me wasn't that he bothered to point out the mistakes; as a journalist, my aim is to be accurate. No, it was the *way* he did it: smarmily, self-righteously, with a sort of how-dare-you-not-care-about-this-as-much-as-I-do attitude. Finally, I'd had it. Beyond this, it'd been a hellacious week at work and my fuse was already short. Now this. I came home, vented to my wife, and told her I was going to email the reader back and share a piece of my mind with him.

"Are you sure you want to do that?" she asked, channeling a bit of Proverbs 15:1. ("A gentle answer turns away wrath, but a harsh word stirs up anger.")

I offered a succinct "Yes," male-speak for "Oh, just let me be *stupid*."

Often I will write an email response to a reader strictly to vent, then, before I press Send, conjure up one of those two-choice computer buttons in my head: "Do you really want to be a jerk and anger this guy even though it's only going to make the situation worse?" The two options: "No. Cancel" and "Yes. Be a jerk right back at him."

I usually press "No. Cancel," but this time I pressed "Yes."

Big mistake. It only made the situation worse. In my response, I acted with all the maturity of a twelve-year-old, telling him to put himself in my shoes and write three columns a week for a decade and not make a single error. "Not one!" I wrote. In terms of immaturity, I did everything but say my dad could beat up his dad, which would have been tough since my father had been dead for years.

My anger raised his. My lamenting on the difficulty of my job triggered his lamenting on the difficulty of his *life*, which was, to be blunt, sad. The pride oozed out of me like a popped blister. I felt small and petty, like Steve Martin in *Planes, Trains and Automobiles* after he rips into John Candy for being a "Chatty Cathy Doll. . . . Here's an idea: Try having a point!" Martin's tirade wounds Candy to his core—and so had mine wounded the reader.

You'd think I would have learned by now: a few moments of righteous-fueled payback only worsens a bad situation. That "gentle answer" verse is spot on. Every time I've resisted returning evil for evil, I've been thankful for making that choice. Every time I've given in to it, I've regretted it.

God is about the people business. The imperfect people business. And if he loves me despite my bad choices, the least I can do is love others despite theirs.

So—am I really raising a glass and saying this? *Here's to Scrooge, the Founder of the Feast!*

The high we get from getting back at someone typically is very short-lived, and we often are more bitter than before! Why is it better to leave vengeance to the Lord (Romans 12:19)?

_____

_____

_____

_____

Think of someone in your life who is struggling with bitterness. What are some gentle ways to model God's love toward them? Ask God for wisdom in helping them overcome their hurt.

_____

_____

_____

You Can't Wish Away the Uncomfortable

Cover them. I do not wish to see them.

—SCROOGE, IN THE 1984 MOVIE VERSION, TO THE GHOST OF
CHRISTMAS PRESENT, AFTER BEING SHOWN IGNORANCE AND WANT,
THE FRIGHTENINGLY UGLY FACES OF NINETEENTH-CENTURY POVERTY

When the Ghost of Christmas Present shows Scrooge two animal-like children the ghost has been hiding in the folds of its robe, the hideous image gets in the face of Ebenezer—literally. They are "scowling, wolfish" figures, Ignorance and Want, symbolic of what can happen when society neglects the poor. Though, given the example of Tiny Tim's virtuous spirit amid poverty, they are not symbolic of what *must* happen to the poor.

"Whose children are these?" asks Scrooge.

"Man's," says the Spirit.

"Have they no refuge or resource?" asks an obviously moved Scrooge.

"Are there no prisons?" mocks the Spirit with words straight from the pre-Ghost Scrooge. "Are there no workhouses?"

The 1984 movie version takes the license to reveal Scrooge's deeper reaction. "Cover them," he says. "I do not wish to see them."

Isn't that the same reaction some of us have when we see the poor on the street corners with their cardboard signs? We don't want to see them. We wish they would either go away or stay at the mission so they'd be conveniently removed from our sight. So, like Scrooge, we wouldn't have to face any responsibility for them—despite numerous Scripture verses suggesting the poor should be a priority with us—or so we wouldn't have to feel guilty for being more fortunate.

What other people do we see as inconveniences instead of opportunities? It's far more comfortable to interact with people who seem to have it together than those who don't, isn't it? To interact with people just like us—the laughable assumption, of course, being that we have it together. People we understand and can relate to.

Jesus, meanwhile, reached out to the lowest of the low—lepers, for example. When seeing Ignorance and Want, His reaction would have been just the opposite of Scrooge's. "Bring them here," He'd say. "I wish to see them."

The Ghost of Christmas Present has been trying to show Scrooge a truth he long ago discarded: he is no better than anyone else. "It may be, that in the sight of Heaven, you are more worthless and less fit to live than millions like this poor man's child," it says to him at the Cratchit house. To expose him to Ignorance and Want is to expose him to society's—and, thus, *his*—penchant to look the other way instead of help.

Says James 1:27, "Religion that God our Father accepts as pure and faultless is this: to look after orphans and widows in their distress and to keep oneself from being polluted by the world."

Too often we label people with baggage as undeserving of our time and attention, when these are the very people who *deserve* our time and attention. People who are needy. People with addictions. People who don't fit elsewhere. To follow Jesus is to try to see the world as He sees it, meaning we take responsibility for the benefit of others. Meaning we embrace the spiritual-village-to-raise-a-child perspective. Meaning we don't look away from need just because to do otherwise is to sometimes feel guilt or shame.

To see the faces behind pain is to realize these are people like you and me. It's easy to ignore prisoners, for example, until you've spent an evening with a support group of friends and family who haven't given up on them. Suddenly you realize how courageous these folks are in their refusal to give up on loved ones who've made terrible mistakes but still deserve support.

Jesus said, "Come to me, all you who are weary and burdened, and I will give you rest. Take my yoke upon you and learn from me, for I am gentle and humble in heart, and you will find rest for your souls. For my yoke is easy and my burden is light" (Matthew 11:28–30).

We, too, should seek to give rest to the weary. And that begins with a willingness to see what's hiding in the folds of the robe.

Are there people you view as inconveniences rather than opportunities? List them here and ask God to change the way you perceive them and to give you creative ways to minister to them.

_____

_____

_____

_____

Charles Dickens wrote *A Christmas Carol* from a nineteenth-century perspective, yet the social ills of Ignorance and Want are still with us today. How do they present themselves in our technologically advanced world?

_____

_____

_____

Fear Has an Upside

Ghost of the Future! I fear you more
than any Spectre I have seen.
—SCROOGE, AS THE THIRD AND FINAL
SPIRIT COMES FOR HIM

The final Ghost has no essence of a child as did the Ghost of Christmas Past nor essence of Christmas as did the Ghost of Christmas Present. Instead, writes Dickens, "it would have been very difficult to detach its figure from the night, and separate it from the darkness by which it was surrounded." This is one scary Spirit, silent though it may be.

No wonder Scrooge's legs "tremble" as he faces the Ghost of Christmas Yet to Come. Yet as the Spirit points a gnarly finger forward, Scrooge doesn't hesitate. "Lead on!" he says. "The night is waning fast, and it is precious time to me."

Though frightened, Scrooge is eager because his encounters with the two other Ghosts have convinced him that this trio of trips is in his best interest. Means to a greater end. Darkness that will lead to some sort of light. In other words, Scrooge is likely thinking, *I'm scared out of my bedroom slippers, but I know this is something I must do.*

"I know your purpose is to do me good," he tells the Ghost of Christmas Yet to Come, "and I hope to live to be another man from what I was . . . and do it with a thankful heart."

Is this the same Scrooge who, early on, wanted to deny these Spirits even existed? Now he's looking expectantly for what he might learn because it will be in his best interest, despite being chilled with fear.

We have seen Scrooge become aware of his shortcomings. We have seen him catch a vision to change. We have even seen him conjure strategies to change: wanting to treat Bob Cratchit and the Christmas-caroling boy better. But the start of stave four presents something else: Scrooge with a passion—and the apparent courage—to change despite a fear of what that might mean.

Have you been there? You desperately want a job you're interviewing for and are wracked with fear each time you think of that interview. You want to get married—and are convinced God would smile on the union—but are afraid you haven't built a wide enough financial base to do so. You desperately want to go overseas and do missionary work but are stymied by fear about trying to break into a culture that's so different from the one you know.

Fear comes in many varieties. We fear we're not good enough, a common problem with new writers I teach in workshops. We fear we'll fail. We fear we'll let others down. To fear is human; to let that fear stifle us from becoming more for God is regrettable.

Lesson 17 discussed the downside to fear. Here are three things that represent its upside.

First, fear is a necessary passageway for us to become more than we are. "The fear of the LORD is the beginning of wisdom," says Proverbs 9:10. We bow to His leading even though we aren't sure where that leading will take us—as Scrooge bows to the leading of the Spirits even though he isn't sure where they will lead him. In both cases, our willingness to follow suggests a faith that dilutes the fear. We may be worried about the journey, but we know that we're on it for a greater purpose. If the steps of life change are awareness, vision, strategy, and courage, achieving the latter becomes possible not because of an *absence* of fear but because we *overcome* that fear. In other words, fear is a necessary passageway through which we must enter—and courage is what allows us to take that first step.

Second, fear is a protection from stuff that can hurt us. When interviewing one of the "Band of Brothers" from World War II, Don Malarkey, I asked about the role that fear played in the men in combat. "I was often fearful," said Malarkey, a technical sergeant in the 101st Airborne Division. "Fear was your friend. Because when you were afraid, you were aware of the enemy. And when you were aware of your enemy, you had a better chance of not getting yourself killed."

Finally, fear is a window into our souls, the illumination of some obstacle we cannot overcome on our own. To whistle in the dark is to rationalize there's nothing to fear; it gets us nowhere. To acknowledge we're afraid but to trust God to overcome that fear—that gets us somewhere.

When confronted by the Ghost of Christmas Yet to Come and his own death, Scrooge isn't afraid of the actual dying but of all the living he's left undone. In the words of Marley's Ghost, "One life's opportunity misused."

So, give credit to Scrooge. He's squirming but still eager to go on this journey of discovery. The key to conquering fear isn't to feel unafraid; it's to step into the darkness *despite* feeling afraid. It's trusting God more than trusting the world.

"There is no fear in love," says 1 John 4:18. "But perfect love drives out fear, because fear has to do with punishment. The one who fears is not made perfect in love."

I was the featured speaker at a Young Life camp in Malibu, British Columbia, when, during lunch, a leader said, "Uh, Bob, we're doing the ropes course right after lunch and we'd like you to be one of the guides up in the trees. It's always good for the kids to see the leaders up there to inspire them."

He might as well have suggested that I walk barefoot across hot coals in front of these kids. I was petrified. Two weeks earlier, at another Young Life camp, I had first been on such a course and, though I did it, I also was shaking in my running shoes. Now I was supposed to be a model of fearlessness to these kids while dangling one hundred feet up in a Douglas fir?

God somehow gave me the courage to dangle high in the trees, helping kids get from one perch to another. Looking back, I have to believe God was taking a weakness of mine and turning it into a strength, making more of me than I would have been had I refused to risk.

Franklin Roosevelt gets all the credit for his famous line from his WWII fireside chats: "The only thing we have to fear is fear itself." But his wife Eleanor's quote about fear is more practical: "You must do the thing you cannot do."

Better yet, check out Deuteronomy 31:6: "Be strong and courageous. Do not be afraid or terrified because of them, for the LORD your God goes with you; he will never leave you nor forsake you."

What overcomes fear? Moving. Daring to go somewhere you've never been, whether it be high in a tree, overseas to a different culture, into a marriage, or, in Scrooge's case, to the unknown outcomes of Christmases to come.

"It's always darkest before the dawn" is a saying we're all familiar with. What does this mean in the context of your daily walk with the Lord?

_____

_____

_____

_____

Why does Scrooge fear the Ghost of the Future more than the other Spectres? What about the future makes us fear it more than the past or the present?

_____

_____

_____

Letting Go Means Grabbing Hold

Lead on! Lead on!

—SCROOGE, TO THE GHOST OF CHRISTMAS YET TO COME

Undergoing life change, whether it be a complete overhaul or minor tune-up, takes more than courage. It takes admitting that you don't have all the answers. That you can't fix yourself. That you might *want* to control your life, but you'd be better off allowing God to take that control.

It's not easy, particularly if your whole life has been about control, which it has for Scrooge. He doesn't want to give up anything. A single shilling to the solicitors for the poor? No! A day off work to Cratchit? No! An ounce of consideration to his nephew? No! Scrooge's whole life is about control. He guards it jealously.

Control. Isn't that what cost him Belle? She dares suggest that his life is out of control; he's reaching for fool's gold. "The master-passion, Gain," she calls it. She challenges him to look at himself objectively, but he chooses otherwise. Why? Because to change means to give up control. To link with another in love is to share control; it's the only way such a relationship can work. And at that point in his life, Scrooge isn't interested.

Thus does he become a small-time puppeteer and Cratchit his leading marionette. He will rule. He will bow to nobody. Instead, others will bow to him.

Never mind that it has left Scrooge miserable. Controllers don't like to look at themselves in the mirror, so they ratchet their control tighter with those who threaten that control. Controllers want to dominate, to control the behavior of everyone, to speak and not listen—and in worst cases, to physically abuse.

"People who feel out of control tend to become controllers," writes Dr. Judith Orloff, a Los Angeles psychiatrist and author. "Deep down, they're afraid of falling apart, so they micromanage to bind anxiety. They might have had chaotic childhoods, alcoholic parents, or experienced early abandonment, making it hard to trust or relinquish control to others, or to a higher power."

Sounds more than a little like Scrooge, especially the abandonment part, since he had been placed in a boarding school by a father whose meanness was implied by his sister's comment that he had suddenly gotten "kinder."

All of which makes Scrooge's acquiescing to the Spirits all the more amazing. With the Ghost of Christmas Past, he "clasped its robe in supplication." With the Ghost of Christmas Present, Scrooge is asked to touch its robe. "Scrooge did as he was told, and held fast," writes Dickens. And to the Ghost of Christmas Yet to Come he now cries, "Lead on!"

The latter is quite the opposite of a control freak's typical behavior. It is giving power to someone else. Trusting someone else. Showing vulnerability. At a deeper level, it is also a cry for help.

A local alcohol rehab center in our community used to run an advertisement that said, "The healing begins the moment you call." And what is calling? It's giving up control. It's admitting you can't heal yourself on your own. It's letting go.

To do so doesn't mean we become God's marionettes; otherwise, why would He have given us freedom of choice? It means we trust Him for the direction in our lives, we follow the advice offered in His Word, and we bow to His authority. It means we've come to the point where we don't have all the answers and are willing to let someone else help us find them.

And if your heart attitude is such as Scrooge's—"Lead on!"—the corollary is fairly obvious: *I am willing to follow.* In our egocentric world, that's often looked upon as weakness. Something negative. A loss. But God isn't interested in us buying into this world; He loves us too much for that. He wants us to buy into Him.

"Do not conform to the pattern of this world, but be transformed by the renewing of your mind," says Romans 12:2. "Then you will be able to test and approve what God's will is—his good, pleasing and perfect will."

In other words, Scrooge is saying to the Spirit, "Your will, not mine."

We should say the same to the Holy Spirit—and see the places that choice will lead.

It's difficult to admit we don't have all the answers. What would your life look like if you had a magical way to get all the answers? How would that affect your reliance on God?

_____

_____

_____

_____

What are some things you need to let go of in your life? Ask God to help you release these things and reveal to you what to grab hold of instead.

_____

_____

_____

Your Life Matters More Than Your Death

*It's likely to be a very cheap funeral, for upon
my life I don't know of anybody to go to it.*

—A BUSINESSMAN, IN REGARD TO SCROOGE'S FUNERAL

As the Ghost of Christmas Yet to Come shows Scrooge a handful of people's reactions to a man's death, Ebenezer is confused. If the Spirit is to illuminate his life, Scrooge wonders, why is he not present in any of these scenes?

"It's likely to be a very cheap funeral," says one man, "for upon my life I don't know of anybody to go to it."

The other suggests he would go, but only if lunch were provided.

At one stop, a trio is going through the possessions of the dead man with a frivolity bordering on sacrilegious. At another, a man is breathing a sigh of relief; he and his wife owed money to a now-deceased man who had been ruthless in his pursuit of it. "It would be bad fortune indeed to find so merciless a creditor as his successor," the man chortles to his wife. "We may sleep to-night with light hearts."

Scrooge is bothered by these people's insensitivity to the dead man, which is interesting on two counts. First, it's yet another reminder that he is softening; would the pre-Ghost Scrooge have cared a wit how people reacted to a man's death? Second, he doesn't appear to realize what is obvious to the rest of us: the man whose death means so little to these people is Scrooge's.

"If there is any person in the town, who feels emotion caused by this man's death," says Scrooge, "show that person to me Spirit, I beseech you."

Then later, as if the truth is becoming more apparent: "Let me see some tenderness connected with a death."

Scrooge using the word *tenderness* in a sentence? As the Spirit floats him from one scene to the next, Scrooge is observing his own funeral, even if he refers to it as "a death" and not "*my* death." And he doesn't like what he sees, which is the embodiment of a line in "Song of Myself" from the poet Walt Whitman: "Whoever walks a furlong without sympathy walks to his own funeral drest in his shroud."

That, of course, leads to a question we all might ask ourselves: What would we want our own funerals or memorial services to look like? What would we want said about us? How would we want people to react?

To ask such questions isn't necessarily to tug on our egos. Realizing that our lives have a finish line that seals our earthly legacy can help us become more like the person we want to be remembered as.

We all want our lives to count for something, even if that realization, for some, is hidden deep inside, obscured by pain, addictions, betrayals, whatever. As such, it's not a bad idea to picture ourselves as Tom Sawyer and Huckleberry Finn, having come back to town to see what folks are saying about us after we're gone.

Better yet: instead of seeing how people react to our *death*, ask how God might react to our *life*. John 12:43 talks about people who "loved human praise more than praise from God."

There's a big difference between the two. The praise of God is consistent, while the praise of man is fickle. How many athletes and entertainers who were stars yesterday have been forgotten today? Heroes to zeroes. One-hit wonders. Has-beens.

What's more, the praise of God is everlasting, while the praise of man is temporary. The Scriptures instruct us to give honor to whom honor is due (Romans 13:7). It's encouraging to hear people at a funeral or memorial service praise someone for a life well lived. But if that's our goal—to earn accolades at our memorial service—then we're shooting too low.

I think of Stephen, in the book of Acts, who is stoned to death for preaching the gospel. Praise from men? He triggers the wrath of men. But just before he dies his lonely death, he forgives those who kill him and speaks of seeing Jesus rising from His throne to welcome him into the kingdom of heaven.

I think of singer Rich Mullins, who died in 1997 at age forty-one in a car accident, such a seemingly inglorious earthly end to a man of such talent, conviction, and compassion. Yet throngs turned out for his service. He was posthumously inducted into the Gospel Music Hall of Fame in 2014, and a full-length feature film, as well as a documentary, were released the same year.

Two faithful men. Two deaths. Two far different responses to their deaths from those on earth, little of which matters in the end. What matters is not who shows up at our service, what people say, and the respect—or lack of respect—they offer. What matters isn't the earthly response to our deaths. Regardless of the response, what matters is how we lived our lives.

This lesson discusses the concept of legacy. What does legacy mean to you, and how has legacy informed your faith journey?

_____

_____

_____

_____

The author discusses the praise of God versus the praise of our peers. What does he mean when he writes that "human praise is fickle"? What are some ways you can experience "praise from God" this week?

_____

_____

_____

Dying Lonely Is the Result of Living Lonely

He frightened every one away from him when he was
alive, to profit us when he was dead! Ha, ha, ha!
—A WOMAN AMONG A GROUP GOING THROUGH THE SPOILS
OF A DEAD MAN WHO TURNS OUT TO BE SCROOGE

The trio pilfering the dead man's belongings knows what this journey with the Spirits has revealed to Scrooge: he is a lonely man.
Make that *was*, since the Ghost of Christmas Yet to Come reminds
Scrooge in stave four that he is, indeed, the man whose death—and
life—people take as a joke.

After look-sees with three different Ghosts, Scrooge has surely seen the lonely man he had refused to face until now. When seeing Belle with her lovingly rambunctious family, he contrasts the fullness of her life with the emptiness of his own. When seeing the Cratchits' joy, he contrasts their riches with his poverty. And now, when seeing the dead man so shabbily treated, he contrasts people's lack of respect with his abundance of regret. It's not hard to put himself in the dead man's shoes—given that they belong to him anyway, as do the feet that go in them.

The results? An utter sense of loneliness.

"If he hadn't been such a wicked old screw"—slang for miser— "He'd have someone to look after him when he was struck with Death," says one of the people going through his items as if at a garage sale's half-off table, "instead of lying gasping out there, alone by himself."

It is easy to tsk-tsk Scrooge's loneliness as that of a miserly man in far-off England in a dark winter long, long ago. Yet here's what Stephen Marche, a writer for *The Atlantic*, said about 2012 America, where some people might have more than a thousand Facebook "friends":

> We have never been more detached from one another, or lonelier. In a world consumed by ever more novel modes of socializing, we have less and less actual society. We live in an accelerating contradiction: the more connected we become, the lonelier we are.

131

We were promised a global village; instead we inhabit the drab cul-de-sacs and endless freeways of a vast suburb of information.

The problem isn't Facebook. Like other technology, social media is a tool that can be used for good—say, raising awareness about a family in crisis that needs support—or for bad—such as frittering away your life looking at what other people are doing instead of going out and building a life of your own. The problem is *us*. People underestimate the value of connections. We either don't value personal connections or we do but aren't willing to help create them.

"You can end up online so much, that you end up sacrificing face-to-face contact," Dr. John Cacioppo, a professor of neuroscience at the University of Chicago who studies loneliness, told Marche. "Having four thousand friends on Facebook might make you feel that you have lots of friends, but you have no face-to-face contact. In that case, loneliness increases."

Meanwhile, we are wired for connection. In Matthew 22:37–39, when Jesus was asked what the most important commandments are, he said, "'Love the Lord your God with all your heart and with all your soul and with all your mind.' This is the first and greatest commandment. And the second is like it: 'Love your neighbor as yourself.'"

We're to be about love. And relationships are to love what airplanes are to flight: they are how we make the phenomenon happen. Families. Friendship. Marriage, if we're so led. Mentors.

Organizations. Churches. Places of work. They're the social web that requires no smartphone, no computer, no apps. They require something far more valuable: us.

Technology is not the panacea some think. Instead, we are finding trends like this: 35 percent of adults older than forty-five are chronically lonely, as opposed to 20 percent of a similar group only a decade earlier, according to a 2010 AARP survey. We have fewer people in whom we can confide; in one survey, the mean size of networks of personal confidants decreased from 2.94 people in 1985 to 2.08 in 2004. What has increased is a reliance on professionals—not friends—to fill the void: social workers, clinical psychologists, family therapists, mental-health counselors, substance-abuse counselors, life coaches—you get the idea.

That's not to say such people can't help; I've benefitted greatly from mentors over the years. But not at the expense of true friendships or a relationship with God through prayer and time in His Word.

Writes *The Atlantic*'s Marche, "We have outsourced the work of everyday caring."

How do you make friends? By taking a risk. Volunteering for an organization. Listening when an acquaintance shares about his or her life. Going to church. Joining a small group. Sending a note of thanks instead of the usual text. Getting off the computer and into someone's life. And heeding some of the best advice I've ever heard: "If you want to make a friend, then be a friend."

Scrooge's life is a bitter argument for the opposite: "Nobody ever stopped him in the street to say, with gladsome looks, 'My dear Scrooge, how are you? When will you come to see me?'" Why? Because Scrooge never stopped to ask the same of them.

As Scrooge could attest, the alternative is a life—and death—of loneliness.

Today's technology makes isolating ourselves very easy. What are some ways you have underestimated the value of connecting with others?

_____

_____

_____

_____

The author writes that "relationships are to love what airplanes are to flight." What can you do this week to give flight to past connections that have since been grounded and perhaps fallen by the wayside?

_____

_____

_____

Pain Is the Privilege of Losing Someone of Great Value

My little, little child! My little child!
—Bob Cratchit, breaking down after visiting
the grave of his son, Tiny Tim, in a scene with
the Ghost of Christmas Yet to Come

Bob Cratchit tries, honest he does. In the Ghost of Christmas Yet to Come's look at what might be, Cratchit wants badly to be strong for the family, to set the example of persevering despite Tiny Tim's death, to roll up his sleeves and get on with his life in the wake of the little boy's passing.

But he can't. Nor should we expect him to. That is the first of three lessons we can learn from how Cratchit deals with his son's death. As Scrooge and the Ghost of Christmas Yet to Come watch, Cratchit arrives home in a "very cheerful" mood despite having just visited the cemetery where Tiny Tim will rest.

"He broke down all at once," writes Dickens. "He couldn't help it."

"My little, little child!" cries Bob. "My little child!"

For a child to die in England in the mid-1800s was not uncommon. The infant mortality rate was high.

A few weeks after my father died unexpectedly at seventy-two, I had a meltdown. And I felt guilty for that meltdown. My wife called our pastor, who was a close friend. Not incidentally, his five-year-old son had drowned years before. Given that, what right did I have to grieve? He had only five years with his son. My brother-in-law had only sixteen years with his younger son, who plummeted into an icy river and died. I had forty-two years with my father. So why couldn't I get over this?

"How long does it take a man with one arm to get over the loss of his arm?" my pastor asked me.

"But," I countered, "though we got along well, my father and I were very different people. I loved him, but he wasn't the hero that some sons see in their fathers. And it wasn't like he was around every day, like a spouse or child or even a close friend."

"He was your *dad*," he said. "Even though the two of you were different, who you are is linked directly to who he was. He will always be part of you. You're flesh of his flesh. So when he's suddenly not around, you're going to feel as if something is missing. Why? Because something *is* missing. And it's okay to miss that something— that someone."

What he was saying is this: *Pain is the privilege of losing someone with great value.* His words helped me understand death in a new way. Don't pity the man who loses a loved one and weeps; pity the man who loses a loved one and *doesn't*.

The narrator writes it well: "[Cratchit] broke down all at once. He couldn't help it. If he could have helped it, he and his child would have been farther apart perhaps than they were."

Although we may not deliberately search it out, pain is an inevitable part of the human experience. Consider the losses from your life, both small and significant. How did the Lord comfort you and what did you learn from those difficult times?

_____

_____

_____

_____

Read Isaiah 43:2, from more than one translation if possible. Why is water such a powerful metaphor in the Bible, and what does this passage reveal about pain and suffering?

_____

_____

_____

Death Is a Comma, Not a Period

*However and whenever we part from one another, I am
sure we shall none of us forget poor Tiny Tim—shall
we—or this first parting that there was among us?*
—Bob Cratchit, to his family, after the boy's death

Cratchit, in the Ghost of Christmas Yet to Come's look at the aftermath of Tim's death, acts just as we would expect him to act: as the living embodiment of one of those tumultuous April days where the skies turn into a spin cycle of sun, rain, hail, whatever. Death throws us into an emotional tizzy—as well it should. What we've lost isn't a sock or an iPhone or a favorite pen. We've lost something that's irreplaceable.

One moment Cratchit breaks down into tears and the next tells his family, "I am very happy. I am very happy!"

Sandwiched between the emotional extremes is an important statement—the second of two lessons involving Tiny Tim's death: the boy needs to be remembered. "However and whenever we part from one another, I am sure we shall none of us forget poor Tiny Tim—shall we—or this first parting that there was among us?"

This might seem like an eye-roller—well, of *course* they aren't going to forget Tim. But some people try to bury the memory of the one they've lost, thinking it will ease the pain. That doesn't work. Some people believe the way to heal after the death of someone close is to pretend the person has never left. That doesn't work either.

It's best to remember the one you've lost and to remember that you still have a life of your own to live.

In an earlier chapter, I mentioned the courage of a young woman I wrote about who lost her husband, her two-year-old daughter, and her dog in an auto accident that she survived. What amazed me about her story—and the reason I write a column about her every year—was that she refused to let the losses define who she was. Instead, she used the losses as a springboard for good, honoring her school-counselor husband by launching a mentoring program to help the same slip-through-the-crack kids he had been passionate about. And by starting a fun run to raise money for the preschool her daughter had just begun attending.

Wow. What amazing perspective amid her grief. What compassionate clarity amid the blur of loss. And this was no small effort: the mentoring program started with a handful of adults who weekly met, one-on-one, with kids who received little support at home. A few years later, the program had blossomed to nearly two hundred such relationships. And have you ever put on a fun run? I have. It is a heap of work and responsibility.

But here's the other side of the story: amid her efforts to honor her husband's life and her daughter's life, she got on with her own. She remarried—one of her husband's best friends, in fact—and started a new family.

She would candidly tell me that a day didn't pass when she didn't think of losing her husband and daughter. Forgetting her losses would serve nobody: not the ones who died, not herself, not the people around her. But to *not* move beyond them would be a disservice to those same people—and to herself.

After the loss of my father, I learned that death can destroy the body, but it cannot touch the things that matter most. Not memories. Not legacies. Not continuation for those left behind.

And that's simply the earthly perspective. The heavenly perspective dilutes death infinitely more. "For God so loved the world that he gave his one and only Son, that whoever believes in him shall not perish but have eternal life" (John 3:16).

In the language of life, death is poignant punctuation that signals a pause, separating two subjects and forever changing the cadence of the words that follow—but also suggesting that the sentence is not over.

For believers, death is merely a transition from one phase to the next. Knowing this, however, doesn't make the loss of a loved one any less profound. What does Scripture assure us about death? If it helps, use a Bible concordance or online search engine to look up *death* or *suffering*.

_____

_____

_____

_____

Is finding closure after a profound loss really possible? Why or why not?

_____

_____

_____

Amid Tragedy, Others Still Need You

He looked at the work upon the table, and praised the industry and speed of Mrs. Cratchit and the girls.

—THE NARRATOR, ON CRATCHIT'S PRAISING FAMILY MEMBERS SHORTLY AFTER HE VISITED TINY TIM'S GRAVE

You gotta love Bob Cratchit. In the Ghost of Christmas Yet to Come scene, Cratchit weeps in front of the family over the loss of Tim and walks upstairs to his son's room. He sits in a chair that belonged to Tiny Tim. Then, "reconciled to what had happened," he goes downstairs and does his best to be a good husband, father, and friend.

He praises Scrooge's nephew, Fred, for expressing his sorrow to

Bob about the passing of Tim. He praises his wife. And he acknowledges that, yes, son Peter is growing up and will soon begin a family of his own.

The common denominator here? He's outwardly, not inwardly, focused. He's not wallowing in his own sorrow, deep though it is; instead, he's lifting up others. "Encourage one another and build each other up," says 1 Thessalonians 5:11. Despite his own grief, Bob Cratchit realizes something easily lost in times of pain: he's needed by others, and others need to see his good example.

Roughly a century after Dickens wrote *A Christmas Carol,* in January 1945, a day of horror shattered the snowy woods of Bastogne, Belgium, for Staff Sgt. Don Malarkey and others in the 101st Airborne. Amid the Battle of the Bulge, their unit was under heavy fire from the enemy. When the mortars stopped pounding, a handful of US soldiers were dead and the snow was bloodied with the blown-off legs of two of Malarkey's best friends.

Afterward, the survivors gathered around a small campfire, some frozen with the proverbial thousand-yard stare, this war having grown cold, grim, and hopeless. In his right pocket, Malarkey's hand was on a pistol. With a pull of the trigger, he knew an "accidental" shot to his foot would give him a get-out-of-jail-free card. A trip back to England. If he was useless as a soldier, his war would be over.

But he didn't pull that trigger. It was decades later when he finally discovered why he did not. "I realized," he said as I helped him write his book *Easy Company Soldier,* "that it would be better for me to take the coward's way out, but worse for those I'd leave behind. We didn't have many leaders beyond me. In short, I was needed."

I have great respect for people who, in the midst of personal chaos, rise up to take care of those around them. I remember interviewing an emergency room doctor who did this on a daily basis. Granted, the person on her operating table wasn't usually someone she knew; still, it was somebody's father, somebody's daughter, somebody's husband, somebody's wife. "I've always felt that the highest respect I can pay to that family is not in grieving for their loved one who's been in an accident, but, instead, to try and save their loved one's life," she told me. "And I can't do that if I let my emotions lead. I need to lead with my head during the surgery and with my heart afterward."

Cratchit takes a similar approach. He is a lowly clerk. He wears threadbare clothes. He has none of Scrooge's clout. But times of crisis reveal our deepest character. In this imagined death of Tiny Tim, we see Cratchit rise to the occasion: not stuffing his emotions totally, but realizing that he needs to be there for others.

Which, of course, begs the question for you and me: When times are tough, are we there for those who need *us*?

Depending on the situation, sometimes you have to lead with your head, not your heart, and vice versa. Think of a time when you had to lead with your head, not your emotions. What did God reveal to you from this experience?

_____

_____

_____

_____

Who are the people who depend on you when times get tough? What have you learned from these relationships? Offer up a brief prayer of gratitude to God for putting these loved ones in your life.

_____

_____

_____

Your Truest Self Is Your Silent Self

Tell me what man that was whom we saw lying dead?
—Scrooge, to the Ghost of Christmas Yet to
Come, after being shown a veil-covered body

It's puzzling that Dickens shares so much of Scrooge's reactions to what he's been experiencing on this Ghost-led tour but allows him to be silent when, in a scene from the future, Tiny Tim has died. Remember, when the Ghost of Christmas Present sees a vacant seat in the Cratchit home, Scrooge is beside himself with grief about the possibility of the boy dying. Yet here we are, that premonition having come to fruition, and Scrooge says nothing about Tiny Tim's death.

Nothing. There's not even a subtle description from Dickens of Scrooge's physical reaction to seeing the Cratchit family in mourning. Instead, oddly, Scrooge worries aloud about his own fate, asking a question that seems out of context given that the scene's focus has been on the loss of Tiny Tim: "Tell me what man that was whom we saw lying dead?"

He's referring to the pre-Cratchit scenes in which Scrooge was shown the shoulder-shrugging reaction of people to a man's death. My read? Scrooge's silence at the passing of Tiny Tim is actually the unspoken revelation that he has finally connected the dots. Not just some of the dots, as he has before, but all of the dots. It's as if, until now, he was too overwhelmed by the snapshots of Belle and the boarding school and the empty chair to see the bigger picture. Too reluctant—or eager—to understand the deeper meaning of it all. Too preoccupied with each individual number to add up those numbers to see the final answer.

But now, seeing the Cratchits without Tim, it becomes clear. Scrooge adds up all the experiences, and the answer is that he's lived a useless life, has died alone, and has the little boy's death to deepen his pain. Before he even begs the question of the Spirit, Scrooge must know who the dead man is. It's him, of course. Dead while living. Dead without a single mourner. Dead without hope—at least he must think so in this moment.

Sometimes we are at our most genuine when we are silent. When we aren't editing our Facebook post to shade ourselves as a little happier or successful or enlightened than we really are. When we aren't trying to convince someone in an argument that we're right and they're wrong. When we aren't concerned about what others think about us but face ourselves for who we really are.

True honesty with ourselves is that last look in the mirror before bed. The waking up in the middle of the night with worries we've shared with nobody. The quiet prayer we share with a God who knows our hearts inside and out and can call our bluff in a nanosecond if we try to con Him.

Thus, when Scrooge asks the question—who is the dead man?—it is with no real sense of drama or anticipation. It is rhetorical, really. Scrooge realizes his has been a life poorly lived. He seems humbled. Heartbroken. Hopeless.

But the story, of course, is not over.

Sometimes silence can be as effective as words spoken aloud. Using Ecclesiastes 3:7–8 as a starting point, look up *silence* in a Bible concordance or an online search engine. What does Scripture reveal?

_____

_____

_____

_____

Scrooge recognizes from his encounter with the Ghost of Christmas Yet to Come that he has been wasting his life on the wrong priorities. What are some of the priorities from your own life that you would like to change? Offer them up to the Lord and ask Him to illuminate the pathways to make that happen.

_____

_____

_____

LESSON 35

Before Honor Comes Humility

Answer me one question. Are these the
shadows of the things that Will be, or are they
shadows of things that May be, only?
—SCROOGE, TO THE GHOST OF CHRISTMAS
YET TO COME, IN THE CEMETERY

This final tour has been a morbid one for Scrooge, filled with death and darkness and regret. The graveyard scene is a bleak one, draped in hopelessness, it would seem, as Scrooge tries desperately to convince the Spirit—and himself—that he's redeemable.

As the Ghost reveals a tattered graveyard and one specific tombstone within, Scrooge all but pleads to avoid a fate that may be inevitable. "Before I draw nearer to that stone to which you point," he says to the Phantom, "answer me one question. Are those the shadows of the things that Will be, or are they shadows of things that May be, only?"

He is the condemned man looking for an eleventh-hour stay of execution from the governor. And when hearing nothing back from the Spirit, he has to be thinking that no news is not necessarily good news. Thus does Scrooge offer a dramatic touch-of-life philosophy, a statement spoken with whistling-in-the-dark wishfulness, as if were he to say it aloud, with feeling, it might just come true.

"Men's courses will foreshadow certain ends, to which, if persevered in, they must lead," he says. The suggestion? He *gets* it: you reap what you sow in life, right? Ah, but if he gets it, he doesn't really want to get it. He wants there to be some sort of loophole, some way out, some magic wand like the Ghost of Christmas Present's torch that can change people's dispositions—or, in this case, a Spirit's mind—on the spot.

Thus does he offer self-spun hope: "But if the courses be departed from, the ends will change. Say it is thus with what you show me!"

In other words: *I don't want to die as a lonely, miserable old man. I can change. Please give me another chance.*

If there is desperation in Scrooge at this point, it is a place where all who change must necessarily get. To make something new, you must rip out the old. And that can look ugly.

If you've ever done a remodel project, you know what I'm talking about. My family lives in a house built in 1939, and remodeling means ripping off walls that expose lath-and-plaster underpinnings. It's ugly. It's depressing. It's defeating. But there's no other way to make it look beautiful than to strip the room to its ugliest during the process. In the same way, there's no way for people who have chosen unwisely to become wise; they often have to hit rock bottom.

Destruction must come before reconstruction. "Come, let us return to the LORD," says Hosea 6:1. "He has torn us to pieces but he will heal us; he has injured us but he will bind up our wounds." And says Proverbs 15:33, "Humility comes before honor."

Pleading with the Spirit in the graveyard, his pride long gone, Scrooge is George Bailey ("I want to live again; please, God, let me live") on the bridge toward the end of *It's a Wonderful Life*.

He's Jean Valjean ("Let him live!") of *Les Misérables*, pleading with God to let "the son I never had" not die from his battle wounds. But the Spirit's finger points to the name on the grave: *Ebenezer Scrooge*.

Scrooge recoils. But he is an irascible old coot and is going to fight this to the end. "Why show me this, if I am past all hope?"

First he defends himself as a changed man. Then he appeals to the Spirit's hoped-for good nature: *If this is the end, hasn't this all been a huge waste of time and effort for you and your Spirit partners?* Now he shifts to promises.

"I will honour Christmas in my heart, and try to keep it all the year," he says, almost like the teenager promising he'll clean his room every day if he can go to the concert.

The Spirit remains nonplussed.

Finally, so desperate is Scrooge to make amends that he morphs from words to action. He tries to grab the Spirit's hand to emphasize how eager he is to "have his fate reversed." But, writes Dickens, "The Spirit, stronger yet, repulsed him."

Or did it?

"Holding up his hands in a last prayer to have his fate reversed, he saw an alteration in the Phantom's hood," writes Dickens. "It shrunk, collapsed, and dwindled down into a bedpost."

A common belief is that people can't change, yet Christianity is all about the changing of hearts. Consider your favorite Bible characters and what they reveal about redemption and transformation.

_____

_____

_____

_____

As Scrooge encounters his own tombstone, he pleads for another opportunity to redeem himself. Have you ever been desperate for a second chance? Did you receive it? Why or why not? What did you learn?

_____

_____

_____

LESSON 36

God Makes Good on His Promises

I am here to-night to warn you that you have
yet a chance and hope of escaping my fate.
—The Ghost of Jacob Marley, to Scrooge

As the fifth and final stave begins, Scrooge is in his bed, repeating his promise to begin anew. The Ghost of Christmas Yet to Come is gone. Scrooge is not lying dead in that graveyard. In fact, you could argue, the man has never been more alive, bouncing around his bedroom in glee.

He exclaims, "I am as light as a feather, I am as happy as an angel, I am as merry as a school boy. I am as giddy as a drunken man."

In short, Scrooge realizes he is a redeemed man. Perhaps it came when he prayed, as the narrator tells us, a "last prayer to have his fate reversed." For whatever reason, he has, indeed, been given a second chance, and his thankfulness gushes forth in unbridled joy. "Oh Jacob Marley! Heaven, and the Christmas Time be praised for this! I say it on my knees, old Jacob; on my knees!"

It's significant that he first mentions Marley. Given all that's happened to Scrooge with the Ghosts of Christmas Past, Present, and Yet to Come, Marley's visit to Scrooge might easily be forgotten. But remember what he had said? "I am here to-night to warn you that you have yet a chance and hope of escaping my fate."

Now that chance and hope have proven true. That possibility has turned into a reality. That promise has been fulfilled.

Promises are cheap these days. Politicians make them to get elected and break them once they're in office. Advertisers make them to get you to buy a product that doesn't live up to its billing. People vow in front of friends and family to love their chosen one despite whatever comes their way, then leave that person for someone else when the waters get choppy.

But God's promises come with no such capriciousness. "For I am convinced that neither death nor life, neither angels nor demons, neither the present nor the future, nor any powers, neither height nor depth, nor anything else in all creation, will be able to separate us from the love of God that is in Christ Jesus our Lord" (Romans 8:38–39).

In other words, no matter how dark the night, you are never without hope when you trust in the Light of the World.

Say what you will about the Ghost of Marley; it pulled through in the clutch. Made good on the promise. Delivered the goods. The Spirit tells Scrooge, in essence, *It's too late for me, but it's not too late for you. You don't have to wear these chains that I do. You can escape my fate.*

Promise.

Have you ever been let down by a broken promise? How did it make you feel?

_____

_____

_____

_____

Romans 8:38–39 assures us that nothing separates us from God's love. How do God's promises differ from human promises? What are some efforts you can make to keep your own promises to others?

_____

_____

_____

LESSON 37

Regret Leads to Renewal

Spirit, hear me! I am not the man I was. I
will not be the man I must have been.

—Scrooge, to the Ghost of Christmas Yet to Come

The Ghost of Marley, on a required mission of sorts, earlier promises Scrooge a hope of redemption. And Scrooge's response to the three-trip lesson has been decidedly encouraging, wouldn't you agree?

Scrooge learns, grows, and exhibits not only a willingness to change but a desperate desire to change. What would his future have been had he laughed off his Christmas-trip trilogy? Who knows? Maybe this was a grace-heavy intervention to begin with; perhaps the Spirits—or whoever is behind the Spirits—had decided Scrooge was going to get a second chance regardless of how he reacted to his experiences.

Again, we don't know. What we *do* know is that the broader perspective instilled in Scrooge something that allows him to change: regret. Genuine remorse for how he lived results in a genuine desire to make amends for it.

Some people equate regret with guilt, an emotion with only a single side—a bad side. But regret is more. It's the rocket booster on a space shuttle that allows the craft to soar to new heights, then detaches from it and falls helplessly into the Atlantic Ocean.

Regret leads to renewal. But it's not something we have to drag along for the entire trip. It's fuel to empower us to new places, a means to an end, and a catalyst to change, but not a ball-and-chain we can never unfetter, à la Jacob Marley. It forces us to face ourselves, inspires us to be more than we were, then falls out of the way—unless we choose to take it with us, in which case it weighs us down in the form of guilt.

How does a wounded relationship heal? By the two parties experiencing regret and using it as impetus for change. How does an alcoholic get well? By channeling regret into new energy to recovery. How does a nonbeliever believe? By admitting past sins and accepting God's forgiveness for a new future.

"Godly sorrow brings repentance that leads to salvation" (2 Corinthians 7:10).

Regret helps us make sense of the world, avoid repeating

mistakes, and gain insight. It's not a fun place to be. Scrooge was in anguish as he cried out to the Ghost of Christmas Yet to Come, "I am not the man I once was."

But in the end, regret helps get him where he needs to be.

What is the difference between regret and guilt when you place them within the context of your own life?

_____

_____

_____

_____

Have you ever had a relationship that got wounded? How did it get wounded and how did God help the wound to heal?

_____

_____

_____

LESSON 38

Denial Prevents Change

It's humbug still! I won't believe it.
—Scrooge, to the Ghost of Jacob Marley

Why does it take Scrooge almost a lifetime before he changes his ways? Because until the Spirits force him to confront himself, he lived, like some of us, in a constant state of denial.

He had worn deep the ruts of rationalization into his life's routine. He had refused to *feel*, lest it bring back all the painful memories of the past. He had learned that if he played the victim card, he could conveniently overlook the needs of others. If he could convince himself that Cratchit wanting Christmas Day off was an abomination against him and his company, then he wouldn't have to face being a stingy old man who hates the idea of anyone else being happy.

Without liquor or drugs, Scrooge has learned to anesthetize himself from the world around him. It protects his pride. It protects his ego. It protects his power. As long as we deny that others might have needs that we could meet, then we don't feel compelled to lift a finger for anyone else.

On the other side of the ledger—a metaphor Scrooge could relate to—denial prevents any hope of us becoming more than we currently are. We remain stuck with ourselves, inflexible, unwilling to consider something new. And if we repeat all this, day after day, it becomes so routine that we don't stop to consider we could live any other way.

What Scrooge needed to do was stop denying the realities of his life and acknowledge that he wasn't king of the universe. "Whoever wants to be my disciple must deny themselves and take up their cross daily and follow me," Jesus said in Luke 9:23.

In essence, that's what "Old Scratch" finally did. And the payoff was nothing less than a new life.

Even Christians can manage to anesthetize themselves from the world's pain and heartache. What are ways you have put your guard up to protect yourself, and what has God given to believers to help them cope with life's difficulties?

_____

_____

_____

_____

Denial is a handy tool for avoiding hard truths. Contemplate a time you were in denial. What did you learn once you were able to confront the truth of the matter?

_____

_____

_____

LESSON 39

Grace Changes Everything

Best and happiest of all, the Time before
him was his own, to make amends in!
—THE NARRATOR, ON SCROOGE'S REALIZATION THAT
HE'S ALIVE AND HAS BEEN GIVEN A SECOND CHANCE

As a moneylender, a man of numbers, Scrooge can do the math. He can add up the number of times he's shooed away solicitors for those in need, the scowls he's offered passersby, the pieces of coal he's hoarded in his office while Cratchit warmed his hands by a candle, the mean-spirited comments he's fired at his nephew Fred, the ice-cold comments he's issued about the poor—and on and on. And what they add up to is this: a man who deserved no consideration. No favors. No second chances.

Yet this is exactly what the Spirits grant him.

In a word: this is *grace*. Undeserved favor.

Scrooge deserved, if not some punishment akin to what Marley has received, to keep dragging around the chains of misery he'd become so accustomed to that he hardly noticed they were there. To simply be left alone, given that his life was seemingly hell on earth, right? Wouldn't that be punishment enough, to leave Scrooge to his utter loneliness, even if he was too proud to admit it? Regret, even if he was too driven to look back? And selfishness, even if he was too blind to see it?

But there he is on Christmas morning, awash in new hope, clicking his heels in the air, anticipating—for the first time in how long?—the day ahead.

Forgiveness will do that to you. It will turn your regret into a rejuvenated spirit. Your shame into a passion to make amends. Your emptiness into a fullness that's irrepressible.

G. K. Chesterton wrote that Dickens "had a sort of literary hospitality; he too often treated his characters as if they were his guests." God does the same thing, though I'm not about to fault Him for doing it "too often." We would be wise to live not only as guests, but as sons and daughters of the One who breathed life into each of us.

As those blessed by God's grace, how easily we forget that we once stood in that dark graveyard with the Spirit's finger pointing at a grave with our name on it. And once were given the same second chance Scrooge was.

Have we forgotten what life was like without God? If so, we should remember, lest we forget how blessed we are. To forget is to overlook how God's grace changes everything—or will if we let it. To diminish how powerful forgiveness is—or should be if we pass it on to others. To ignore how freeing mercy is—or can be if we continually let Him work through our lives instead of returning to our Scrooge-like world of scowls and ledgers.

Let Scrooge's newfound zest be a reminder of what we have lost. If we've grown numb to such goodness, may we rejoice in Scrooge's new life. And let us begin each day, as he does for the first time, being reminded of how rich we are in God's grace.

Hebrews 4:16 mentions God's "throne of grace." The idea of an awe-inspiring throne room combined with the concept of undeserved favor paints a compelling juxtaposition of power and mercy. How does God use power and mercy in our lives to draw us closer to Him?

_____

_____

_____

_____

Think of a time you deserved punishment but received grace instead. What did God reveal to you from this experience?

_____

_____

_____

LESSON 40

Let Your Heart Be Light

*Really, for a man who had been out of
practice for so many years, it was a splendid
laugh, a most illustrious laugh.*

—THE NARRATOR, ON SCROOGE'S REACTION TO HIS NEW LIFE

In realizing his newfound freedom, Scrooge notices, and appreciates, that he's been given a second chance. He vows to live in the past, present, and future. He offers praise for the turnaround, wonders what he should do now, revels in his joy, and—get this—*laughs*.

Yes, Scrooge laughs.

"Really, for a man who had been out of practice for so many years, it was a splendid laugh, a most illustrious laugh," Dickens writes splendidly.

Ecclesiastes 3:1–4 reminds us:

> There is a time for everything,
> and a season for every activity under the heavens:
> a time to be born and a time to die,
> a time to plant and a time to uproot,
> a time to kill and a time to heal,
> a time to tear down and a time to build,
> a time to weep and a time to laugh,
> a time to mourn and a time to dance.

This isn't Scrooge's time to die or to weep or to mourn. He just went through a three-Ghost Ironman course that tore him down to his naked soul. And now his slate has been wiped clean.

So, yes, now is a time to laugh. It is a time to dance, which brings to mind Belle's question in the 1984 movie version: "When was the last time you danced?" It is a time to live out Job 8:21: "He will yet fill your mouth with laughter and your lips with shouts of joy."

Twenty-five years ago, when our family moved to the city where we now live, relatives invited us to attend the church they attended. We did so and never left. Later I was asked what drew me to this particular church. I knew they were expecting a "churchy" response such as, "We felt the Holy Spirit alive" or "God's Word was preached with unequivocal integrity." Something like that. Instead, I was honest.

"The laughter," I said. "People laughed a lot. That seemed really healthy to us."

I'm not naive. Laughter alone isn't the barometer for church health. And we take church seriously. But laughter, on top of lots of other good things, certainly is. I am suspicious of speakers, writers, and other influencers who don't laugh—because, biblically, we're told this is to be part of who we are. And if we, like Scrooge, have been graced with new life, shouldn't one of our expressions of that grace be laughter?

The new Scrooge certainly thinks so. Still, we're encouraged to approach life with a touch of levity, when circumstances allow.

"There is nothing in the world," Dickens once said, "so irresistibly contagious as laughter and good humor."

Who are we to doubt him?

Read Genesis 21:1–6, the passage in which Sarah has a son in her old age and names him Isaac, which means "He laughs." Why should we consider laughter a wonderful gift from God?

_____

_____

_____

_____

Who are some people in your life who could use a good laugh? Ask God for some creative ways to tickle their funny bone this week.

_____

_____

_____

LESSON 41

There's Joy in Starting Over

I'm quite a baby. Never mind, I don't
care. I'd rather be a baby.
—SCROOGE, IN THE JOY OF HIS DISCOVERY
THAT HE'S ALIVE AND WELL

The three sentences are mixed in with dozens of others that express Scrooge's exuberance on this new day and might easily be overlooked. They should not be. Not only because of what they suggest but because of their context.

My apologies to vegetarians among you dear readers, but the three sentences are the juicy meat of a spiritual sandwich: the pieces of bread on either side being the laughter just mentioned and the sound of church bells ringing, far different than the ominous bells that rang in Scrooge's house before the Ghost of Marley appeared. No, these Christmas morning bells were "the lustiest peals he had ever heard . . . Oh, glorious. Glorious!"

In between? Scrooge's suggestion that he has been born anew. "I'm quite a baby," he says.

Could there be a more incongruous statement from the man? First, consider the simple reality-of-age argument. Though the narrator never reveals Scrooge's age and some have estimated it as a mere fifty-seven, he seems old. "He was . . . a grasping, scraping, clutching, covetous old sinner!" writes the narrator. Second, he abhors the innocence of youth. He is about as kid-friendly as a porcupine. And he is fueled by a subtle grown-up pride that grates against anything exuberant—goodness, remember how he lambasted his nephew for his Christmas cheer?—and anything that is fresh, new, and innocent.

But now Scrooge utters the words, "I'm quite a baby." (Significant, by the way, is the fact they echo Dickens's favorite verse from Scripture, Matthew 18:3: "Verily I say unto you, Except ye be converted, and become as little children, ye shall not enter into the kingdom of heaven" [KJV].) Scrooge then pauses at the thought, almost as if wondering, *Did I really just say that?* As if, though he's been made new, he still has a recollection of the man he once was. Then he says this: "Never mind, I don't care. I'd rather be a baby."

If it is an odd wish, perhaps it is an odd wish that more of us should consider. "Like newborn babies, crave pure spiritual milk, so that by it you may grow up in your salvation," says 1 Peter 2:2.

The suggestion isn't that we stay as babies; Hebrews 5:13–14 points out milk is for babies and solid food "for the mature, who by constant use have trained themselves to distinguish good from evil." God expects us to grow and to mature in discernment and knowledge. But we should never stop longing for "pure spiritual milk."

Never stop appreciating the fresh slate that God's grace offers us, the kind of each-day-a-wonder sense of a child. Never stop remembering that, if we have accepted God's grace, we are born anew.

To which we should respond with Scrooge's unbridled joy: "Hallo! Whoop! Hallo here!"

The Christmas season tends to bring out the child in all of us, just as it did in the novel, when Scrooge gets a second chance at life. What are some of your favorite childhood memories of Christmastime?

_____

_____

_____

_____

Think back to the time when you were a "baby Christian" in your walk with God. How has your faith matured and evolved over time? Are there areas that still need maturing? Ask God to show you pathways to a deeper faith.

_____

_____

_____

LESSON 42

You Must Be Present to Win

Running to the window, he opened it, and put out his head. No fog, no mist; clear, jovial, stirring, cold.
—SCROOGE, ON CHRISTMAS MORNING

In these moments of exhilaration, Scrooge is understandably consumed with his new lease on life. Like the athlete who's just scored a touchdown or netted a three-pointer at the buzzer, he's reveling in the moment. You can almost imagine him high-fiving the three Christmas Spirits and offering the Ghost of Marley a festive fist pump. But then he heads to the window and looks outside to the city beyond, to the "golden sunlight," to the "heavenly sky."

He moves from self to the world at large. He craves perspective.

And he acquires it two ways: first, by broadening his vision beyond himself, then by asking a question.

When I teach writers' workshops, I remind students that writing doesn't begin at the keyboard. Nor does it begin at the research stage or even at the hatch of an idea. "Writing," I tell them, "begins with who you are as a person and what you notice in the world around you. You cannot be a writer unless you *notice*."

That's what Scrooge suddenly feels compelled to do when he goes to the window: notice. Because to notice is to open ourselves to all sorts of potential that otherwise lies dormant. To notice is to see. To see is to feel. To feel is to build connections with those around us. And to build connections with those around us is to fulfill God's co-priority for us: "Love your neighbor as yourself" (Matthew 22:39). The other, of course, is to love God.

In other words: *you must be present to win*.

Remember the stave one Scrooge? The last thing he wanted was perspective, connections, to *feel*. "External heat and cold had little influence on Scrooge," writes Dickens. "No warmth could warm, nor wintry weather chill him."

Now he's opening the window to all sorts of new possibilities.

Beyond noticing, the second way he broadens his perspective is by asking a question. To my journalism students, I would categorize this as research. "What's to-day?" he calls out to a boy in his Sunday clothes.

"To-day! Why Christmas Day."

Instead of inquiring about how someone else is doing, how often do we check in and check out of church with robotic cadence, saying our hellos and smiling and nodding but never taking time to ask someone with the actual intent of finding the answer: "How are you doing?" Which might lead to, "How can I help? How can I pray for you?"

Like many, I'd rather stay cocooned in my comfort zone than risk asking those questions. But when I have ventured to ask, I'm always amazed at how eager people are to have someone take an interest in them. Once, after noticing how a video shown in church of a husband and wife having an argument had moved a young man to tears a few rows ahead of us, I approached him after the service.

"You okay?" I asked this guy I did not know.

Those two words led to an outpouring of grief as he recounted having just gone through a painful divorce and feeling hopeless that he would ever find someone to love. They also led to a friendship between the two of us, to the man getting involved in men's ministries, and to him doing repair work on my pickup. (As I write, he has remarried and the two of them are expecting their first child.)

For writers, noticing and asking questions is how we collect the ingredients that we're going to use to concoct whatever meal we're going to offer readers. For people in general, noticing and asking questions are how we build the relationships that God says should be the priority of our lives.

Warning: When you open that window, it can be risky. It might not be a sunny Christmas morning out there; it might be a gray, boring January day. Freezing rain might pelt you in the face like cold bullets. You might not like what you see. But the alternative is to wrap ourselves in our cocoons, never venturing out and never getting the chance to fulfill our purpose for being alive.

The author tells his writing students, "You cannot be a writer unless you notice." Change one word in that sentence: "You cannot be a *Christian* unless you notice." Why is noticing such an important part of our faith walk and how we interact with others?

_____

_____

_____

_____

The best thing about being in our comfort zone is the comfort, of course, but that doesn't serve us or others very well. How does God use discomfort not only to change us but also the people we encounter in our daily lives?

_____

_____

_____

Give Because You've Been Given To

Go and buy [the turkey] and tell 'em to bring it here,
that I may give them the directions where to take it.
—SCROOGE, TO THE BOY ON THE STREET BELOW

Now we can add *perspective* to the list of gifts that Scrooge inherits with his new life. But there's one more gift that may be more important than all the rest: *action*. He takes initiative for the benefit of others. He instinctively realizes that he must give away the benevolence that he, himself, has been accorded.

First, he asks the boy to fetch a prize turkey from the poulterer for the Cratchit family. What's more, he promises to tip the boy half-a-crown if he can have the bird to him in five minutes or less. (I can hear the 1843 commercial now: "We deliver in five minutes or less, or your turkey is free!") Upon the boy's arrival, he realizes the turkey will be burdensome for the lad to carry, so he calls for a cab.

This three-act scene—turkey, tip, cab—is hugely significant. Why? It is the first act of kindness we've ever seen Ebenezer Scrooge offer. Now, it's true that he gave Bob Cratchit Christmas Day off, but only grudgingly, grousing that it wasn't fair or convenient and was the equivalent of picking a man's pocket. And only after demanding that Cratchit come in all the earlier the next day to compensate. That's hardly *kindness*.

It's true, also, that while traipsing around with the Christmas Ghosts, Scrooge feels concern for others, Tiny Tim in particular. He feels remorse for the way he treated a couple of people, regret for having let the pursuit of gain sever his relationship with Belle, and respect for his old boss, Old Fezziwig, for putting on the Christmas party to benefit his employees. But the turkey scene is the first time Scrooge actually *acts* upon an emotional impulse. "Dear children, let us not love with words or speech but with actions and in truth," says 1 John 3:18.

Thinking good thoughts about the poor doesn't put a meal in front of them. Waving a flag but doing nothing to contribute to your community reflects shallow patriotism. And lavishing praise on an employee at her going-away party is too little, too late if she hasn't been given, at best, an occasional bonus over the years—or, at worst, an occasional email saying, "Good job."

We are what we do. When writing a feature story about someone, I long ago learned you consider only lightly what people say about themselves or what others say about the subject. Instead, if you really want to find who your subject really is, you look for what he or she *does*. Action speaks louder than words.

Love may begin with a feeling. Scrooge's calling a cab for the little boy because the turkey would be too heavy for the lad to carry may well have been the man's first expression of empathy— identifying with someone else's feelings or difficulties. But feeling sorry for someone and doing something to help that person are two different things. Scrooge's feelings led to actions, completing the circuit and bringing a touch of goodwill to the world.

When we hear the word *love* we're apt to think of some blissful feeling and a couple strolling hand-in-hand in the park. But love, at its deepest, is better shown by images of sacrifice, long hours worked, meals cooked, and personal pursuits forgone for the advantage of another. It is seen in forgiveness, in a willingness to listen, perhaps even in a parent loving his or her child enough to say no. It is better manifested in flying across the country every other week to spend time with a sister dying of cancer. In a missionary toiling in the shadows of a remote village to teach someone the grace of God. Or in the nails of a cross.

But foundational to any act of love is action, a physical doing for others as thanks to God for what He's already done for us.

The turkey scene near the end of the novel is important because it shows that Scrooge has changed from within. What does the scene tell us about the need for action versus mere platitudes in our daily faith walk?

_____

_____

_____

_____

Love is much more than just a romantic feeling. It has many facets, including agape love, which is defined as "unselfish concern for the good of another." What are some small yet meaningful ways you can express agape love to someone this week?

_____

_____

_____

LESSON 44

Don't Give Expecting to Receive

I'll send it to Bob Cratchit's. He
shan't know who sends it.
—SCROOGE, REGARDING A SURPRISE GIFT

If you want a litmus test for whether Scrooge is truly a changed man or just going through the motions—whether he's truly concerned for others or simply thrilled that he's cheated death—this is it. Not only does he immediately decide to honor, with a turkey, the clerk he's treated so shabbily, but he wants to do so without taking credit for the gift.

"He shan't know who sends it," says Scrooge with a touch of glee.

That decision shows a maturity that far surpasses the biblical Pharisees, who considered themselves righteous and benevolent

185

but were frauds right down to their designer sandals. Jesus chastises them for being hypocrites who "love to pray standing in the synagogues and on the street corners to be seen by others" (Matthew 6:5).

Dickens had no patience for hypocrites. "I have always had, and always shall have, an invincible repugnance to that mole-eyed philosophy which loves the darkness, and winks and scowls in the light," he once said in a speech.

"Dickens," writes Michael Heard, author of *The Annotated Christmas Carol*, "believed in good works, not just good words. His was an active Christianity that had no place for hypocrites."

In *A Christmas Carol*, the Ghost of Christmas Present offers a passionate putdown on those who don't walk the talk. "There are some upon this earth of yours who lay claim to know us," the Spirit says, "and who do their deeds of passion, pride, ill-will, hatred, envy, bigotry, and selfishness in our name, who are as strange to us and all our kith and kin, as if they had never lived."

Jesus, on the other hand, healed a blind man at Bethsaida and charged His disciples "not to tell anyone about him" (Mark 8:30).

"Be careful," he said in Matthew 6:1–2, "not to practice your righteousness in front of others to be seen by them. If you do, you will have no reward from your Father in heaven. So when you give to the needy, do not announce it with trumpets, as the hypocrites do in the synagogues and on the streets, to be honored by others."

Like Scrooge, we must be about the deed, not the credit. About the heart, not the headlines.

Scrooge's desire to give anonymously reflects the purity of his heart, his motives, his concerns. The gift is all about the Cratchits, not about him.

The pay-it-forward movement rests on the same principle. You've heard the stories: at a restaurant drive-through people in one car pay for the meal of the folks in the car behind them, a complete stranger pays ten thousand dollars so a woman can have a liver operation she could not afford, and churches "adopt" the sons and daughters of prisoners to make sure they all receive Christmas presents.

The joy isn't in the being recognized for giving. The joy is in the giving, period.

A joy that Scrooge is experiencing for the first time ever.

Jesus encouraged anonymous generosity because he understood that giving unselfishly has the power to heal the giver as well as the recipient. What are some creative ways you can bless someone without bringing attention to yourself?

_____

_____

_____

_____

Read Matthew 6:5–8. Jesus essentially says in verse 7 that we should keep our prayerful words to a minimum because "your Father knows what you need before you ask him." Write down five simple prayers you can offer up to the Lord this week. Try to keep each one at ten words or fewer.

_____

_____

_____

Giving Changes Your Perspective

What a delightful boy! It's a pleasure to talk to him.
—SCROOGE, ON CHRISTMAS MORNING, TO
THE BOY OUTSIDE HIS WINDOW

If Scrooge's giving nature is a sign of how he has changed, then another sign is his perspective on life in general. And there's a connection between the two: when we give, we look at the world and the people around us with different eyes. We even look at ourselves with different eyes.

We see it first in Scrooge's interaction with the boy who's fetching the turkey for the Cratchit family. Amid his conversation with the young man, Scrooge says, "An intelligent boy! A remarkable boy!" And moments later: "What a delightful boy! It's a pleasure to talk to him."

Are you kidding me? Ebenezer "I Wish to Be Left Alone" Scrooge is finding pleasure in *something*, particularly something related to another human being?

It's true. Scrooge once looked for the worst in people; now he looks for the best. In people. In everything. The knocker on the door about which "there was nothing at all particular" at the story's beginning now holds a sudden fascination with him as he awaits the boy and the turkey. "I shall love it, as long as I live!" he says, patting it with his hand. "I scarcely looked at it before. What an honest expression it has on its face! It's a wonderful knocker!"

It's the equivalent of George Bailey kissing the once-despised newel post that won't stay put on the staircase, after he'd returned from his life-changing time travel with the angel. Like Scrooge, he's a changed man after the angel helps him change his perspective on life.

It's not only Scrooge's outlook on people and things that changes but his disposition itself. When he dresses, he looks "irresistibly pleasant" and is so quick with a smile to those he meets on the street that people return the gesture in kind. The "Merry Christmases" and "Good mornings" are coming from people fast and furious, which thrills him to his all-new core.

Too often, in our modern world, the opposite plays out. An uncaring person yammering on a cell phone cuts off another driver. The other driver responds with a honk or obscene gesture or a shout of disdain, perhaps a trifecta of returning evil for evil if all three are involved. And the world is the worse for it, such incidents occasionally resulting in physical violence.

But when we soften our hearts and consider the needs of others, it changes who we are as people. And it changes others in the process. Do you see the storyline here? Scrooge regards others with kindness. Others respond with kindness to Scrooge. The world is better for everyone.

All of which bears out a biblical truth we dare not ignore: giving changes our perspective on everything. "It is more blessed to give than to receive," Jesus said in Acts 20:35. And a big part of that blessing is the perspective to appreciate more deeply those around us.

Have you ever found yourself looking for the worst in people, in spite of what the Bible says about such pessimistic behavior? How and why does this outlook affect the pessimist worse than it does the object of derision?

_____

_____

_____

_____

Christmas is a wonderful time not only for being introspective about the past year but also for looking outside ourselves and discovering the God-given potential in others. Who needs uplifting in your life and how can you encourage them?

_____

_____

_____

LESSON 46

Seeking Forgiveness Is a Sign of Strength

[Scrooge] is my name, and I fear it may not be pleasant to you. Allow me to ask your pardon.
—SCROOGE, ON CHRISTMAS MORNING, TO ONE OF THE
MEN HE'D REFUSED DONATIONS TO THE PREVIOUS DAY

When it comes to giving, some things are easier than others. While we can admire Scrooge for having the turkey sent to the Cratchits, tipping the boy, and getting the lad a lift, that really doesn't cost him much, does it? Even smiling and wishing folks a Merry Christmas, while nice, isn't a big sacrifice. But then Scrooge sees one of the two men who had come by his place of business the previous day, seeking money for the poor. Scrooge, you'll recall, rebuffed the two with less tact than a nightclub bouncer.

The difference, of course, is pride. It's far easier to give when it costs us only money or time or effort. But when it costs us pride, that's another matter, because we guard our egos tenaciously. If we've been hurt by another, it costs us pride to accept their apology. And if we've hurt someone, it costs us pride to offer an apology.

But Scrooge doesn't hesitate after the man recognizes Ebenezer as the one who treated him and his fellow solicitor so coldly the previous day. The old Scrooge would have done more than hesitate; he probably wouldn't have even recognized the man or, if he had, ignored him, fearful of being hit up once again. The new Scrooge, when the man recognizes Ebenezer, mentions his name and says, "I fear it may not be pleasant to you. Allow me to ask your pardon."

If anyone had doubted Scrooge's sincerity of his about-face in life, this would convince them that he's not just blowing smoke. And what he does next would seal the deal: he backs up his sentiment with sacrifice. He tells the man he would now like to donate to the cause of the poor, the first time in the story when he steps up to meet the needs of the masses—perhaps with an image of Ignorance and Want in the back of his mind.

Note, too, that he does not shout the amount from the rooftops, or even loudly enough to catch the attention of passersby. Instead, says the narrator, Scrooge whispers it to the man, pointing out that the large amount—"My dear Mr. Scrooge, are you serious?"—included "many back payments." In other words, he would do what he could not only to *say* he was sorry but to *show* he was sorry, to make amends for his stinginess in the past with not mere lip service but show-me-the-money action.

The next morning, when Bob Cratchit arrives to work, Scrooge's apology represents works, not words. He raises the clerk's salary substantially and wishes him a Merry Christmas. He offers assistance to the Cratchit family, presumably in financial aid to Tiny Tim, who, we are told, does not die. He insists Bob buy more coal to keep the office warmer. And he invites the clerk to join him for a bowl of smoking bishop—a popular tavern drink consisting of red wine poured on ripe bitter oranges.

All these actions are to say *I'm sorry*.

"The weak can never forgive," said Mahatma Gandhi in *An Autobiography: The Story of My Experiments with Truth*. "Forgiveness is the attribute of the strong."

Doing so is hard enough when we know, as Scrooge does, that we have wronged someone, harder still when two have wronged each other—and each might be waiting for the other to go first.

Indeed, there may be no greater measure of a person's character than to have the courage to seek forgiveness and to have the grace to accept it. Shortly after this, Scrooge goes to church. While this, too, is a big step for a man who probably had not gone in decades, it is not the equal of forgiving. It is quite easy to play church, to go through the motions, to not get involved, and to walk away feeling as if we've done our duty. No such wiggle room exists in the world of forgiveness.

"Forgiveness is the name of love practiced among people who love poorly," writes author Henri Nouwen. "The hard truth is that all people love poorly. We need to forgive and be forgiven every day, every hour increasingly. That is the great work of love among the fellowship of the weak that is the human family."

And on this Christmas morning, Ebenezer Scrooge seems to be saying for the first time, *I want to be part of that family.*

Why is forgiving someone who wronged you an act of strength, not weakness?

_____

_____

_____

_____

Social media has highlighted the phenomenon of the "humblebrag" in which someone draws attention to what would otherwise be considered an act of modesty, humility, or generosity. How does humblebragging undermine the act of forgiveness as we understand it in Scripture?

_____

_____

_____

LESSON 47

It's Not About the Ghosts

I will live in the Past, the Present, and the Future.
The Spirit of all Three shall strive within me.
I will not shut out the lessons they teach.
—SCROOGE, TO THE GHOST OF CHRISTMAS YET TO COME

It's not about the Ghosts.

As we finish Scrooge's amazing journey, we have to understand that these are not rely-on-us-to-save-you Spirits. These are means-to-an-end Spirits. What's important is not the Ghosts, per se, but their lessons, the truths they illuminate. And Scrooge seems to get this when he promises the Ghost of Christmas Yet to Come that he will "not shut out" the lessons the Spirits have taught him.

And what, in summary, are those nuggets of wisdom?

The Ghost of Christmas Past teaches Scrooge an array of lessons, among them that facing our pasts can be impetus for changing our futures. Scrooge doesn't start out as a bitter, penny-pinching lout. Despite a challenging childhood, he becomes a well-grounded young man who'd met a well-grounded young woman. But he loses himself—and a vision for others—to the insidious idols of money, materialism, and—Belle's description—"Gain." He loses the beauty of *feeling*. His return to the boarding school and Belle and the Fezziwig party remind him of love, wonder, delight, family, community, fun, levity—things that he'd once experienced but had slipped away, emotions that had once infused him with life but now lay dormant, and connections to the heart stuff of life that had become disconnected. So the Ghost of Christmas Past teaches him perspective on himself.

Next, the Ghost of Christmas Present teaches Scrooge perspective on the people around him—how those with so little, such as the Cratchits, can have so much; how much joy he was missing, such as the lively party at nephew Fred's house; and how our choices affect other people. When the Spirit tells Scrooge he sees a vacant seat in the Cratchit home "if these shadows remain unaltered by the Future," Scrooge realizes that he has the wherewithal to help save the boy. And when the Spirit unveils Ignorance and Want, it hammers home the idea that we have responsibilities to society at large.

Finally, the Ghost of Christmas Yet to Come underscores how much we can matter. Tiny Tim dies, in part, because of Scrooge's not stepping forward to help. And in the people's ho-hum reaction to Scrooge's death, we realize how little we *might* matter.

When given a second chance, though, Scrooge proves himself worthy of it.

To honor the Ghost of Christmas Past, he no longer worships at the idol of gain. He *feels* again. When he invites Cratchit for a bowl of punch and says, "Make up the fires, and buy another coal-scuttle before you dot another i, Bob Cratchit," he sounds just like his old boss, Fezziwig: "Clear away, lads, and let's have lots of room here! . . . Chirrup, Ebenezer!"

To honor the Ghost of Christmas Present, he bonds with the larger community, goes to church, begins giving to the fund for the poor, and looks in the eyes of people he passes, smiling and wishing them good morning and Merry Christmas.

Finally, to honor the Ghost of Christmas Yet to Come, he not only saves the life of Tiny Tim by giving money for his care, but he becomes like "a second father" to the boy.

Like Scrooge, we gain perspective from considering the past, the present, and the future—even if we are to live in the now. As believers, our story is rooted in the past: Jesus was born, showed us how to live, died for our sins, and rose again, giving us hope of everlasting life. Our story plays out in the present, where, like Scrooge, we are called to fling open the windows of possibilities, hit the streets, and make a difference in the lives of others. And, finally, our story plays out in the future, where our hope lies in a heaven to which entrance is based not on a standard of good and bad, but on God's grace to forgive us and on our willingness to accept that grace.

It's not about the Ghosts.

Yes, it's important to live in the now, but life also includes the past and the future. How do the past and the future inform the way you lead your life in the present?

_____

_____

_____

_____

Read Exodus 3:14. When God said, "I AM WHO I AM," He essentially declared that He was not bound by time or space, that He was eternal. As His children, we, too, are eternal beings. How does this knowledge affect the way you see yourself? How you see others? How you live your faith?

_____

_____

_____

Life Is Best Lived Imaginatively

I can make this into anything I want it to be:
a baseball bat, a whip handle, the spoke of
a ship's wheel, taking me to new lands.
—BENEDICT SLADE, IN THE TV MOVIE VERSION *AN AMERICAN*
CHRISTMAS CAROL, TO AN ORPHAN HE BEFRIENDS IN THE FINAL SCENE

As an expression of Dickens's classic, *An American Christmas Carol*
does grand justice to the story and hits me at a deeper emotional level
than any of the other films. In particular, I'm touched by a final scene
that bookends the story, wherein Benedict Slade, the movie's version
of Scrooge, hands a piece of wood to a young man at an orphanage.

Early in the movie, Slade was that orphan, and he had a piece
of wood handed to him with the encouragement of making it into

something more. Now, after his life runs aground on the shores of materialism and he's had his life-changing romp with the Ghosts, he returns to the furniture factory and offers the young man an apprenticeship. To make a point, he hands the boy a piece of wood and asks him if he knows what it is.

"It's a stick," says the boy.

No, no, no, Slade corrects. "I can make this into anything I want it to be: a baseball bat, a whip handle, the spoke of a ship's wheel, taking me to new lands."

The point: imagination is powerful. It can take us all sorts of places. Slade is imaginative in even vowing to resurrect the burned-down factory. He's looking not only at what *is* but at what *might be*.

Imagination is the ability to visualize: the ability to form images and ideas in the mind, especially of things never seen or experienced directly. And it's integral to us in living up to our potential.

"A vision is a clear mental picture of what could be, fueled by the conviction that it should be," writes Andy Stanley in *Visioneering*.

God's imagination is always at work. He took nothing and made it into something: the universe, complete with people, nature, animals, even that wild-looking blobfish. He took people whose potential others did not see, and imagined the leaders they might be: Moses, David, Peter, and dozens of others. And, daily, he takes us where we are and nudges us to be more than we might otherwise be—for His glory.

Writes Oswald Chambers, "In intellectual matters you can think things out, but in spiritual matters you will think yourself into cotton wool. If there is something upon which God has put His pressure, obey in that matter, bring your imagination into captivity to the obedience of Christ with regard to it and everything will become as clear as daylight."

Dickens channeled his imagination not only into writing books but into his vision for making the world a better place. "His mind was full of possibilities," writes Michael Hearn in *The Annotated Christmas Carol*.

But the pre-Ghost Scrooge? "He lacks imagination," writes Hearn, "as it might distract him from making money."

On the other hand, when used for more constructive purposes, imagination helps get Scrooge from thinking he is a hopeless loser to thinking he could be a born-again difference maker. Imagination helps us see others not for who they are but for who they have the potential to be. Imagination helps us get from wherever we might be mired to some promised land beyond.

When the Ghost of Christmas Past gives Scrooge a chance to reclaim his lost innocence, he does so by redeveloping his imagination. "Memory plus imagination prompts compassion—itself a form of imagination," writes Norrie Epstein in *The Friendly Dickens*, "since it allows us to transcend ourselves and feel what others feel." Another example: Until the Ghost of Christmas Present gives Scrooge a glimpse of the Cratchit family, Ebenezer never imagines that Bob had a real life outside the office. To Scrooge, Cratchit was nothing more than his personal pencil pusher who raises the limits of in-office coal consumption. And when the poor remain faceless—when we don't imagine the struggles they face—it is far easier to think of them as only "surplus population."

Imagination, then, becomes leverage for something as complex as a life change or as simple as appreciating the beauty of the earth. "If we are children of God, we have a tremendous treasure in Nature," writes Chambers. "In every wind that blows, in every night and day of the year, in every sign of the sky, in every blossoming and in every withering of the earth, there is a real coming of God to us if we will simply use our starved imagination to realize it."

It's not only the stuff of fairy tales. Said Albert Einstein, "Knowledge is important but imagination is essential."

So, here, take this stick. What can you make of it?

One has only to look at a platypus to understand that God has a vast imagination (and a pretty good sense of humor)! Why do you think God imbued his human creation with the gift of imagination?

_____

_____

_____

_____

Like muscles, tendons, and ligaments, our imaginations need to be stretched and exercised regularly. What are some ways you can tone up your imagination "muscles" this week?

_____

_____

_____

Redemption Is About Changed Hearts

*It was always said of him, that he knew
how to keep Christmas well, if any man
alive possessed the knowledge.*

—THE NARRATOR, ON THE CHANGED SCROOGE'S
NEW PERSPECTIVE ON LIFE

If *A Christmas Carol* is about redemption—and I believe it is—then what is the catalyst for Scrooge's redemption? It almost sounds like a trick question since lesson 47 ("It's Not About the Ghosts") goes into great detail about how each of the Spirits influenced Scrooge. But the Spirits didn't actually *change* Scrooge; they only enlightened him.

Oh, you might argue, his *circumstances* changed him. He comes home on Christmas Eve a bitter old man and goes through an emotional Ghost blender that purees him into a softened soul by Christmas morning.

Actually, when the last Spirit is finished with him, Scrooge's circumstances haven't changed in the least. He is still Ebenezer Scrooge, moneylender, boss to Bob Cratchit, uncle to Fred, dweller in the drafty old house of his former partner. He is the same age, has the same body, and has the same capacity and freedom to think or not think, to feel or not feel. Though the Spirits have some amazing powers, including the Ghost of Christmas Present's cool torch of generosity, none of them instills any superpowers into the old geezer.

So why, at book's end, does the narrator tell us the man has gone from the city's greatest hater of Christmas to its greatest lover of Christmas? "It was always said of him, that he knew how to keep Christmas well, if any man alive possessed the knowledge."

Because Scrooge's *heart* changed, that's why. More specifically, he humbled himself to *allow* his heart to be changed. Treated to fresh perspectives on his past, present, and future, he submitted himself to the Spirits' leadings and, in the end, chose to change. Or, in more theological words, he *repented*—the necessary bridge between regret and salvation.

Fred says in the story's beginning that Christmas inspires people to "open their shut-up hearts freely." That's exactly what Scrooge is doing now: opening his shut-up heart freely.

"With power must come an inner sense of connection to others that, in Dickens's life and work, comes from the model of Jesus Christ as benevolent Savior," writes Jane Smiley in *Charles Dickens*. "The truth of *A Christmas Carol* that Dickens understood perfectly and bodied forth successfully is that life is transformed by an inner shift that is then acted upon, not by a change in circumstances."

We live in a post-Christian world that puts its eggs into three basic baskets: political, material, and self.

The latter is decidedly dependent on a self-determination that suggests we can either bully our way into a new model of ourselves or, with enough social media skills, convince ourselves and others that we are new and improved.

The political basket suggests our contentedness depends on who gets in office, which party gains power, and what bills get passed. Roles change every few years, winners gloating, losers badmouthing, and everybody pretty much ignoring a truth that transcends it all: our contentment or discontentment lies far beyond politics to who we are as human beings, how we live, what we trust, and where we place our faith.

Money and materialism represent the third basket that invariably disappoints. We think that buying things or amassing fortunes will bring us contentment, but they do not; the empirical evidence suggests as much and so does the research. The Ghost of Christmas Present argues the point well while looking in on Christmas celebrations. The poor, despite squalid conditions, are often as content (or more content) than the rich, who have much and, instead of resting contentedly in that, pine for more. Recently, at a social gathering, I heard of a wealthy new home owner who forced painters to redo a room a dozen times. That is not the embodiment of contentedness but an expression of discontentedness on steroids.

Smiley's thesis abides. We aren't changed by circumstances, in this case material circumstances; we are changed by inner shifts. Personal shifts. Heart shifts.

Redemption Is About Changed Hearts

The author defines *repentance* as "the necessary bridge between
regret and salvation." Think of a time when God led you to the
bridge of repentance. What got you there in the first place and what
did you learn from the situation?

_____

_____

_____

_____

Read Matthew 6:25–34, the well-known passage about "the birds
of the air" and the "flowers of the field." What does this scripture
reveal about how we should respond to the temptation toward
materialism and the need to accumulate "stuff"?

_____

_____

_____

LESSON 50

Live with the End in Mind

Oh, tell me I may sponge away
the writing on this stone.

—Scrooge, to the Ghost of Christmas Yet to
Come, upon seeing his name on the headstone

The Ghost of Christmas Yet to Come frightens Scrooge into realizing that life is precious. There is a finish line. You leave nothing to the world but a legacy. Wrote Shakespeare in *Macbeth*, "This life . . . is but a walking shadow; a poor player, that struts and frets his hour upon the stage, and then is heard no more."

For the first time, Scrooge looks at life as something that comes to an end. And that makes him desperately want an altered life—a chance to go back and live it right this time. When his wish comes true, Scrooge throws himself into making amends for his previously wasted life. He'd seen his name on a headstone, a reminder of how fleeting are the years—and how pallid is his legacy. The vision was an embodiment of James 4:14: "What is your life? You are a mist that appears for a little while and then vanishes." A rich man, says James 1:10, "will pass away like a wild flower."

We each will leave a legacy. Like boat wakes, we leave one whether we want to or not. The only question is, what kind of legacy will it be? The answer lies in the choices we make today, tomorrow, and every day that follows.

Imagine you're told you had only six months to live. Would you live differently than you live now? Most will answer that question with a yes. With so little time left, it's important to make the most of it. I get that. What I don't get is why it takes a death prognosis to convince us we should change our priorities. Last time I looked, the chance of each of us dying is 100 percent, which sounds like a death prognosis to me. So why would we not want to wait to live the most meaningful life we could live—and start now?

In the course of *A Christmas Carol*, Scrooge moves from selfishness to regret to repentance to salvation. He gets a second chance. ("God forgive me for the time I've wasted," he tells Fred when showing up unexpectedly on Christmas Day in the 1984 movie version starring George C. Scott.)

Remember, earlier, my mention of the fifty octogenarians who were asked what they would change about their lives had they the chance to live it over again? Among the three: do more things that would live on after they were gone.

That's exactly what Scrooge does: given a second chance, he saves a boy's life, he opens his pockets to the poor, he revels in the giving spirit of Christmas, and he proves to be "better than his word."

If we still have breath, we, too, can change our legacies if we decide to.

As someone once said, the best time to plant a tree was fifty years ago. The second best time is now.

Contemplating our own death may seem morbid, but as the author says, "the chance of each of us dying is 100 percent." Looking back on the decisions you've made—in other words, your legacy—what would you change? What would you keep the same?

_____

_____

_____

_____

At some point, our entire life will be distilled down to a single punctuation mark—the dash between the years on our grave marker. What will your dash communicate to your loved ones? To your friends? To the world in general?

_____

_____

_____

LESSON 51

It Is Never Too Late to Change

He became as good a friend, as good a master,
and as good a man, as the old city knew.
—The narrator, on the new Scrooge

If this book were named *One Overriding Lesson from A Christmas Carol*, that lesson would be this: it is never too late to change. But the choice is ours. God washes us in enough grace to cover our sins "as far as the east is from the west" (Psalm 103:12). He never establishes a you-must-be-this-good-to-make-it-to-heaven edict. But he forces no one to choose His ways.

Instead, He lets us decide.

Scrooge, with a little help from his Spirit friends, ultimately chooses to change. He chooses generosity over selfishness. He chooses people and relationships over money and materialism. He chooses joy over bitterness.

I know someone who has chosen otherwise. I don't say this derisively—and, frankly, I think he would probably heartily agree—but in many ways, he is a modern-day (old) Scrooge. He is bitter about his body breaking down. He is bitter about not being accorded the respect he believes he deserves by certain people. He is bitter about relationships that have not worked out but feels no responsibility to try and repair. He is bitter about people who have wronged him in business.

Beyond all this, he lacks a *purpose* in life. "I don't think it's fair that we should have to live past about age seventy," he told me. When I pointed out that I knew lots of people eighty-plus who were living vibrant, fulfilled lives, he rolled his eyes. When I suggested he volunteer to read to children, he recoiled. "I hate children," he said. When I suggested he spend more time with his grandchildren, he said—half joking, half not—"I don't even know some of their names."

Finally, I realized the loving thing was not to let him sink deeper in this quicksand of pity. As the Spirits did for Scrooge, the loving thing was to help him see himself for who he was: a man who'd done some great things for our country, for our community, and for me, but was now dragging around the chains of regret like Jacob Marley. But not a man without hope.

"You're choosing to be miserable," I told him. "You talk about all the things that haven't worked out in your life instead of reveling in those that have. You've made a difference on this earth. And you can continue to. But you've given up. But God hasn't given up on you."

Subconsciously, perhaps I was channeling Marley's Ghost telling Scrooge he still had hope. Or, better yet, channeling St. Matthew, who recorded the words of Jesus: "Ask and it will be given to you; seek and you will find; knock and the door will be opened to you. For everyone who asks receives; the one who seeks finds; and to the one who knocks, the door will be opened" (Matthew 7:7–8).

I wish I could convince him that he doesn't have to live as a prisoner to doubt, bitterness, regret, self-pity, addictions, and all the more acceptable excuses for unhappiness, such as Scrooge's all-purpose pursuit of "Gain." I wish I could convince him that he needn't drag around those chains.

None of us lives totally unfettered. I think of a young man I know whose addiction led to the loss of his marriage, then his home, then his job. But here's what he didn't lose: hope in the One who can heal. The kid owned his mistakes, dug deep into God's grace, and at a recent writers' workshop got up in front of nearly fifty people and read one of the most courageous reflections on life I've ever heard. Just one of many ways I've seen him emerge as an example of breaking the chains.

God gives us the gift to set ourselves free. Why would we not want to open that gift?

It Is Never Too Late to Change

Being a believer is very much about discovering the joy of freedom that God gives us in abundance. What are some of the freedoms you've enjoyed since your faith journey began?

_____

_____

_____

_____

Do you know someone who has settled for a life of bitterness and self-pity? Though it may seem daunting, what truths can you speak to this person to help them not give up, see past their own misery, and embrace a life of joy and freedom? Ask God for the right words to say in gentleness and love.

_____

_____

_____

LESSON 52

Be the Change You Want to See

We are all charmed with your Carol, chiefly, I
think, for the genuine goodness which breathes
all through it, and is the true inspiring angel
by which its genius has awakened.
—LORD FRANCIS JERRY, IN A LETTER TO DICKENS
AFTER *A CHRISTMAS CAROL* WAS PUBLISHED IN 1843

As he said in the beginning, Dickens wanted not to simply serve up a festive holiday dish with the book. He wanted this book to have an afterlife. He wanted to influence people.

He succeeded.

In the nearly 180 years since it first appeared, the book has never gone out of publication. On Amazon.com, you can choose from more than a hundred variations of the Dickens story. And though some scholars refuse to take it seriously, it is one of the most enduring—and endearing—books ever written, routinely topping lists of readers' favorite Christmas books.

"Its cheery voice of faith and hope, ringing from one end of the island to the other, carried pleasant warning to all," wrote Dickens biographer John Forster soon after *A Christmas Carol* was published.

The British aristocracy did not warm to it. British novelist Sir Edward Bulwer-Lytton huffed that its "fierce tone of menace to the rich is unreasonable and ignorant." The religious press essentially ignored it, finding it too secular for their easily agitated taste. In a classic case of swallowing the camel and sifting the gnat, the *Christian Remembrancer* used the phrase "extreme irreverence" to describe the author's reference to the founder of Christmas having once been "a child himself." *Really?*

But most people see in *A Christmas Carol* not only an interesting read but personal inspiration. The dour Thomas Carlyle, reported *Fraser's Magazine* in 1844, was a Scotch philosopher who did not keep Christmas. "On reading the book," said the magazine, "[he] sent out for a turkey, and asked two friends to dine."

When Dickens read *Carol* aloud in Boston in 1867, the head of a scale-manufacturing business was so moved he immediately lifted the edict of having the plant work on Christmas Day and provided turkeys to all employees. Captain Corbett-Smith read the tale to the troops in the trenches of World War I, more than half a century after it was published.

"It is impossible to read, without a glowing bosom and burning cheeks, between love and shame of our kind, with perhaps a little bit of misgiving," wrote Thomas Hood in *Hood's Magazine*.

In England and the United States, the book helped return the Christmas season as one of merriment and festivity. Dickens and Christmas became almost inseparable. "Even in his own lifetime, he was regarded as the presiding genius of the season of comfort and joy," wrote G. K. Chesterton in 1905. After Dickens died, the poet Theodore Watts-Dunton recalled walking down Drury Lane in London and overhearing a young girl say, "Dickens dead? Then will Father Christmas die too?"

So, what do we do if we, too, find the story has moved us? In a word, *something*. Literature is at its best not only when it stirs us but when we take whatever stirred us and channel it into change for our own lives. That is the ultimate compliment to an author: not that a story moved us but that it moved us to *action*.

It is easy to expect change in others. It is less comfortable to expect it in ourselves. Scrooge went through the wringer before he discovered a new self. Might we, too, avail ourselves to a touch of painful self-discovery to find a richer *us*?

"It seems that in every attack Dickens makes upon society he is always pointing to a change in spirit rather than a change in structure," writes George Orwell.

Change—true change—begins not with political oomph that forces people to comply to some letter-of-the-law edict, but with personal renewal that sees the betterment of the whole in the conviction of the individual. "The solution was psychological, not political," writes Hearn. "The individual can correct injustice. Why wait for society to do it?"

In other words, be the change you want to see.

Just as Dickens's story was written in response to the pessimism of his time and the darkness of a world where children were used as work pawns, so do we have plenty to overcome. Christmas has become so commercialized that few can even remember the way it once was. Hearts have become, like Scrooge's, hardened. Peace and goodwill struggle to keep a foothold amid homelessness, child abuse, and terrorism.

Even if, like some, you find *A Christmas Carol* heavy on caricatures, find Scrooge's conversion unbelievable, and find the threat of Tiny Tim's death, as one critic said, "hitting below the sentimental belt," you can't deny that the book provokes contemplation about our lives.

Orwell suggested that Dickens's characters "never learn, never speculate." But Hearn, the author of *The Annotated Christmas Carol*, disagrees. "This is not true of Ebenezer Scrooge. He *does* learn, he *does* speculate as he heads toward his inevitable redemption. The story's purpose is to record the regeneration of a lost soul; it is a one-character narrative revealed through the mind of this individual."

And once he learns, he assimilates his goodness into the culture around him; he becomes the "salt" and "light" of Matthew 5:13–16.

Dickens paints the old Scrooge as if, like Marley, he were "dead as a doornail," but at least in Spirit, he offers the hope that we can all change. "It is apparent that despite his bilious cant, Scrooge was not completely free of the Christmas Spirit," writes Hearn. "It just lay dormant within him. So little was needed to revive it."

What lies dormant within each of us? A need for connection, perhaps? For belonging, for relationships, for concerning ourselves less about what we don't have than about what others might need?

"*A Christmas Carol,*" writes Epstein, "leaves us, or should leave us, with an apocalyptic sense of urgency to love our neighbors before it's too late."

Indeed, may the thought "haunt" us "pleasantly," and, if necessary, allow us, like Scrooge, to awaken one morning to life anew.

Christmastime and *A Christmas Carol* undeniably go hand in hand.
What are some other Yuletide-related things (movies, foods, books,
songs, TV episodes) that you can't live without each year? What
makes them special?

_____

_____

_____

_____

Of course, Christmas celebrates the birth of the One who gives
each and every one of us the chance to experience life anew, just
as Scrooge discovers for himself at the end of the novel. List five of
your favorite Bible passages that bring to mind the true meaning of
Christmas. Offer a brief prayer to the Lord for giving the gift of His
Son.

_____

_____

_____

Bibliography

Analyzing literature is like fixing a five-course meal for a dinner party: you immerse yourself in the possibilities, research what others have served in similar situations, and sample some dishes that might work. Then, between menu, ingredients, and execution, you imbue your unique stamp on the meal as a chef and present it to your guests, with hopes they will like it.

Or so I would assume, given that the only culinary offering I've concocted with more than two ingredients is a s'more—and that has only three.

My point: As writers, we blend what others have done before us with whatever uniqueness we can bring to the table. Thus, each of our offerings is, at the same time, completely *ours* and completely dependent on others, a hybrid of us and them. It is no different from the twenty-plus movie versions of *A Christmas Carol*: each based on the same story but each with a style, tone, point of view, and cinematic essence all its own.

What I've tried to do is create nuggets of Bible-based wisdom gleaned from an 1843 book that's applicable to our lives today. The recipe might look like this: blend one Scrooge and four Ghosts, seasoned lightly with Christmas. Add one cup human kindness. Mix in New International Version Scripture. Garnish with a touch of humor, a dash of cold-hard reality, and a sprig of holly.

From whence did my ingredients come?

The first thing I did when immersing myself in this project was try to understand Charles Dickens the best I could—not so much as a writer, but as a human being, because who we are as writers ultimately goes back to who we are as people. I refamiliarized myself with books of his I'd read, such as *Great Expectations* and *A Tale of Two Cities*, and got to know ones I had not: *Oliver Twist* and *Nicholas Nickleby*, for example, which reminded me of his compassion and concern for the poor.

To fine-focus on Dickens as a person, I relied heavily on G. K. Chesterton's *Charles Dickens, the Last of the Great Men* (New York: The Press of the Readers Club, 1942). Chesterton's analysis comes from someone who was a great Dickens admirer, a great thinker, and a great philosopher on faith. Chesterton was born four years after Dickens died. In his book, he plumbs the Dickens waters at such depth that, at times, I confess, I struggled to follow him. But the book is punctuated with great wisdom and great wit, including

Chesterton's quote that "the pessimist can be enraged at evil. But only the optimistic can be surprised at it."

Gary L. Colledge's *God and Charles Dickens: Recovering the Christian Voice of a Classic Author* (Grand Rapids: BrazoPress, 2012) offers a more translucent view, particularly in terms of the author's spiritual essence. From a decidedly academic slant, the book twines what Dickens believed, spiritually, with what he wrote.

Dickens's own *The Life of Our Lord: Written for His Children During the Years 1846 to 1849* (New York: Simon & Schuster, 1934) is a rare look at the man's spiritual scaffolding. These are the very words he chose to share with his children about the Jesus he knew and loved and, thus, helped me understand the faith-based underpinnings of *A Christmas Carol*.

Meanwhile, Jean A. Fischer's *A Charles Dickens Devotional* (Nashville: Thomas Nelson, 2012) plies spiritually imbued life lessons from the spans of Dickens's work that I found helpful.

With amazing breadth and a wonderful sense of whimsy, Norrie Epstein's *The Friendly Dickens* (New York: Viking, 1998) helped me understand Dickens the man, Dickens the writer, and Dickens the legend. Epstein presents the author almost as if he were a pop star, which, in some ways, he was. And beyond analysis of *A Christmas Carol* and the author of it, Epstein offers wonderful bits of *Christmas Carol* trivia, not the least of which is that, for the 1938 movie, Lionel Barrymore was originally cast as Scrooge but gave way to Reginald Owen for health reasons. Scrooge and Old Man

Potter (*It's a Wonderful Life*, 1946): what a double billing that would have been!

Oswald Chambers's *My Utmost for His Highest* (Westwood, N.J.: Barbour and Company, Inc., 1963) was a great source for Bible-based wisdom, including His call for us, in lesson 15, to live with "reckless joy." Henri J. M. Nouwen's *The Only Necessary Thing: Living a Prayerful Life* (Chestnut Ridge, NY: Crossroad, 1999) gave breath to my lesson 46 quote, "Forgiveness is the name of love practiced among people who love poorly." And Andy Stanley's *Visioneering* (Colorado Springs: Multnomah, 1999) helped me understand faith in action in a way I'd never quite understood before. "Vision," he writes in what turned out to be prophetic regarding Scrooge's turnaround, "is a clear mental picture of what could be, fueled by the conviction that it *should be.*"

In terms of understanding *A Christmas Carol*, Michael Patrick Hearn's *The Annotated Christmas Carol: A Christmas Carol in Prose* (New York, London: W.W. Norton & Company, 1976) is without equal. Not only does it go into mouthwatering depth on mince pies, death masks, and the roots of the name Cratchit, but the lengthy introduction is chock-full of nuances from, and reactions to, *A Christmas Carol*.

My quotes from *A Christmas Carol* are from *The Christmas Books: Volume I* (New York: Penguin, 1971), a reprinting of *A Christmas Carol* that was originally published in 1843.

Among other books I used for research: Grace Moore's *Charles Dickens' A Christmas Carol* (St. Kilda, Victoria, Australia, 2011); Stephen

Bibliography

Skelton's *Charles Dickens' A Christmas Carol: Special Church Edition* (Nashville, 2007); Hesketh Pearson's *Dickens: His Character, Comedy & Career* (New York: Harpers & Brothers, 1949); and Jane Smiley's *Charles Dickens* (New York: Viking, 2002).

Steve Marche's article on Facebook in the May 2012 issue of *The Atlantic* provided wonderful fodder for my argument that in real modern-day America or fictional nineteenth-century England, loneliness is loneliness.

For lesson 50, Tony Campolo's audio sermon "If I Had to Live It Over Again" (https://soundcloud.com/tonycampolo/if-i-had-to-live-it-over-again) enlightened me about perspective on life.

For weeks, our two-person household experienced a sort of "Christmas in July" movie festival, which included Henry Winkler in *An American Christmas Carol* (1979); Jim Carrey in *Disney's A Christmas Carol* (2009); *The Muppet Christmas Carol* (1992); Alastair Sim in *Scrooge: A Christmas Carol* (1951), perhaps the scariest of the bunch and including a wealth of imagined detail on Ebenezer's past; and *A Christmas Carol* (1938) starring Reginald Owen.

Laugh if you will at the kid comedies in that bunch, but remember what the narrator—a.k.a. Charles Dickens—of *A Christmas Carol* told us: "I should have liked, I do confess, to have had the lightest license of a child, and yet been man enough to know its value."

Acknowledgments

To my friends at Thomas Nelson who've made the *52 Little Lessons* series so much fun and so much better: Kristen Parrish, Heather Skelton, Jennifer Stair, Katy Boatman, and Tiffany Sawyer . . . To my editors at home who've made the book so much better: Fred Crafts, Keith Kessler, Ann Petersen, Dean and Lou Rea, Deena Welch, and Judy Wenger . . . And to the one who endured and encouraged my literary trip back to nineteenth-century London despite my occasional Scrooge-like mood shifts: Sally Jean . . . *I am here to-night to warn you that you have yet a chance and hope of escaping my fate.* No, wait, that's channeling the Ghost of Jacob Marley! I actually wanted to use words from Tiny Tim: *God bless you, every one!*

About the Author

Bob Welch is the author of twenty books. In nearly four decades in the newspaper business, he twice won the National Society of Newspaper Columnists' best-column award. He does inspirational speaking across the country. Welch has served as an adjunct professor of journalism at the University of Oregon and is the founder and director of the Beachside Writers Workshop. He and his wife, Sally, live in Eugene, Oregon.